The Cartoon Old Testament

Cartoons and Commentary on the Old Testament

for additional copies of this or other fine cartoon items,
please visit the official Cartoon Gospel website at:

CartoonGospel.Com

or the main website at:

The-Cartoonist.Com

First Printing June 2011
ISBN: 9780984887200

Published by
Diesslin Press, Dayton, Ohio
info@the-cartoonist.com

Preface

This commentary explores Old Testament scripture passages from the common lectionary through the use of cartoons and musings. The passages are in biblical order by book, chapter and verse, however the lectionary three-year cycle is referenced at the end of the book.

Why Cartoons? A cartoon is somewhat like a visual form of parable. A parable is a short and entertaining story with a message. The idea behind a parable is that the listener will enjoy it enough to remember it and retell it to others (just think if they had e-mail in 800 B.C.E.!). There are parables in both the Hebrew Scriptures (Old Testament) and New Testament, perhaps none more well known than those told by Jesus. Humor, in general, goes a long way toward illustrating a point, often more effectively than serious discourse.

Adam and Eve provide a running commentary at the bottom of each cartoon. This idea began in a prior book *A Journey Through Christian Theology* (Fortress Press) when author William P. Anderson suggested that we needed a way to provide context for the cartoons, in case they were read apart from the text. Adam and Eve became our commentators of choice because of their unique place in human history. In addition, I claim cartoonist's privilege - which simply means that silly things like time, space, history, etc. are all there for me to distort and play with tongue-and-cheek.

The "musings" section provides some extra context. The goal is to deliver maximum insight in minimum space (per the one-page per passage format of the book). I highly recommend keeping a good commentary or study Bible handy for those occasions when your curiosity is peaked and you would like to have a more in-depth understanding.

My deepest thanks go to my wife Mindy for her support and encouragement on this book and all my cartooning projects. It would never have happened without her! She has often been my sounding board for cartoon wording and drawing issues, providing a valuable sanity check to my work. Her mom, my Mother-in-Law, Doris Anne Onken has been particularly helpful in editing this volume as well as being very supportive of this rather off-the-wall second career of mine. In addition, there have been several people who have encouraged and assisted me along the way. Rather than embarrass them here, I'll wait for a more opportune time. However, if it were not for their insights and critiques I may never have stumbled into the current format.

Most importantly, I thank God who blesses us with an abundance of grace. I have come to a deeper understanding of the scriptures and a deeper relationship with God than I had before I started. I guess I will always think of Jesus' teachings as the cornerstone of my understanding of who God is, but I now have a much deeper appreciation of the God who has been there all the time, in the Old Testament and beyond, to the extent we could see it!

I am a cartoonist by profession and a theologian and writer out of necessity. The cartoon is my main medium of expression and therefore my intent is for them to convey, in a memorable and entertaining way, the main points of these scriptures. Thank you for reading the Cartoon Old Testament - I hope it entertains you and enriches your spiritual life.

Rich Diesslin
Cartoonist
M.A. Theological Studies University of Dayton

Table of Contents

Genesis

Genesis 1

Primal Soup to Nuts

In the beginning when God created the heavens and the earth, 2 the earth was a formless void and darkness covered the face of the deep, while a wind from God swept over the face of the waters. 3 Then God said, "Let there be light"; and there was light. 4 And God saw that the light was good; and God separated the light from the darkness. 5 God called the light Day, and the darkness he called Night. And there was evening and there was morning, the first day.

Big Bang or ...

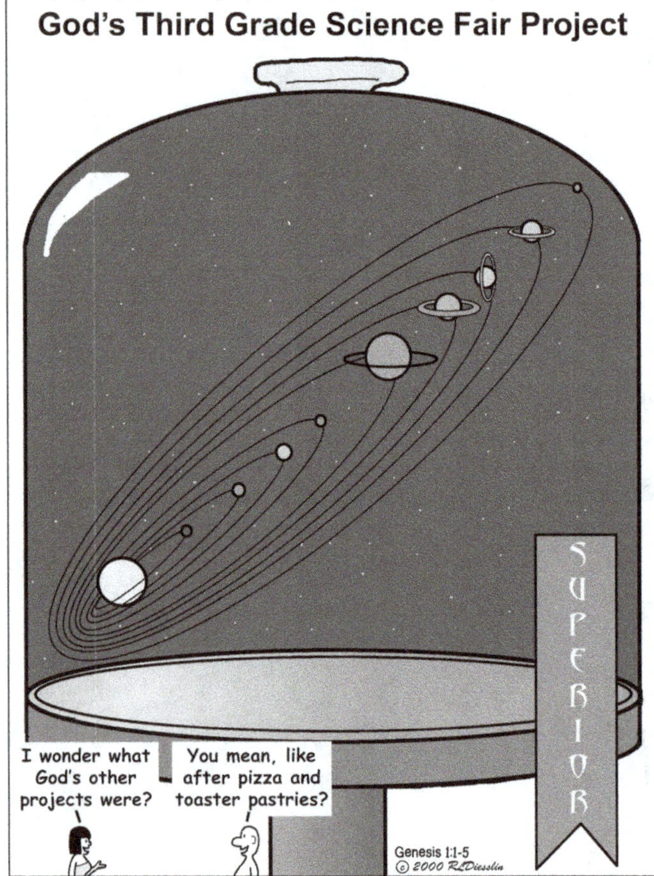

Musings

There are two plausible translations of verse one. The one above and "When God began to create the heaven and earth." This one leaves creation much more open-ended.

The cartoon may bring to mind all sorts of theological questions - "Who was God's third grade teacher?" "Can God be taught?" "Wasn't God here before all else?" "Just why are toaster pastries so good?" This simply means you are forgetting that Cartoonist's privilege sometimes trumps theological concerns and you are taking this way too seriously! But good for you for thinking outside the bell jar. Now from a scientific perspective it has been pointed out the solar system would never align like this (the bell jar would fall over or we'd be sucked into Neptune), that Pluto is not a planet (preposterous) and the spacing is all wrong (but it lays out nicely). So, this brings up another aspect of cartoonist privilege - science is no sacred cow either.

However, while the cartoons will try to find some humor in these verses, most also attempt to show something of theological value. In this case, God is so awesome that perhaps creation of the universe might just be one of those things God did one day when bored. We are so humanity-centric that we can't help but think the universe revolves around us, but science and theology both tell us otherwise. Reading the whole first creation story (all of Genesis 1), can put you in awe of its insight into the ordering of the universe and its origin. You don't need to be a creationist to see God's hand in creation!

Genesis 2:4-9

A Second Creation Story - Adam and Eve

[4] These are the generations of the heavens and the earth when they were created. In the day that the LORD God made the earth and the heavens, [5] when no plant of the field was yet in the earth and no herb of the field had yet sprung up--for the LORD God had not caused it to rain upon the earth, and there was no one to till the ground; [6] but a stream would rise from the earth, and water the whole face of the ground-- [7] then the LORD God formed man from the dust of the ground, and breathed into his nostrils the breath of life; and the man became a living being. [8] And the LORD God planted a garden in Eden, in the east; and there he put the man whom he had formed. [9] Out of the ground the LORD God made to grow every tree that is pleasant to the sight and good for food, the tree of life also in the midst of the garden, and the tree of the knowledge of good and evil.

Adam's Creation - The Cartoonist's Version

Musings

This is the second creation story. Humans, male and female, were created in Genesis 1 and it was very good. So for those with a "humans are basically good" understanding of the Bible, Genesis 1 is for them. For those looking for more of an anecdotal "how humans messed up" approach, they find more material in this second creation story. Here it all starts out innocently enough. Adam (which means earthling or earth creature) is created from the earth and put in a nice garden. As in Genesis 1 God creates and it is good. There's a nice garden, a couple interesting trees, probably a sunny day. What could go wrong!?

Genesis 2:15-25

Eve Arrives

15 The LORD God took the man and put him in the garden of Eden to till it and keep it. 16 And the LORD God com-
manded the man, "You may freely eat of every tree of the garden; 17 but of the tree of the knowledge of good and evil
you shall not eat, for in the day that you eat of it you shall die." 18 Then the LORD God said, "It is not good that the man
should be alone; I will make him a helper as his partner." 19 So out of the ground the LORD God formed every animal
of the field and every bird of the air, and brought them to the man to see what he would call them; and whatever the
man called every living creature, that was its name. 20 The man gave names to all cattle, and to the birds of the air, and
to every animal of the field; but for the man there was not found a helper as his partner. 21 So the LORD God caused
a deep sleep to fall upon the man, and he slept; then he took one of his ribs and closed up its place with flesh. 22 And
the rib that the LORD God had taken from the man he made into a woman and brought her to the man. 23 Then the
man said, "This at last is bone of my bones and flesh of my flesh; this one shall be called Woman, for out of Man this
one was taken." 24 Therefore a man leaves his father and his mother and clings to his wife, and they become one flesh.
25 And the man and his wife were both naked, and were not ashamed.

Boy Meets Girl

Musings

Most parents know if you put a young child in a room with a toy and say "you can do anything you want but don't play with that toy," they are going to play with that toy. However, all is still well. Adam's naming stuff, getting lots of company and God, not Adam, decides he needs a partner. Enter Eve. Adam is ecstatic, but I'm not so sure the other animals aren't just a little bit jealous. One assumes that all the creatures had partners too, but that really doesn't contribute to the story until Noah and the flood. Humans being made male and female from the start (Genesis 1) makes more sense from a creation point of view, but this does explain nicely how we seem to be short a rib and it also establishes that Adam and Eve are made for each other. Also of note - nakedness is no big deal. Adam and Eve aren't really any more self-aware than the other animals, although Adam and God are working on names together.

Genesis 3:1-7

Why You Shouldn't Trust a Talking Serpent

Now the serpent was more crafty than any other wild animal that the LORD God had made. He said to the woman,
"Did God say, 'You shall not eat from any tree in the garden'?" 2 The woman said to the serpent, "We may eat of the
fruit of the trees in the garden; 3 but God said, 'You shall not eat of the fruit of the tree that is in the middle of the gar-
den, nor shall you touch it, or you shall die.'" 4 But the serpent said to the woman, "You will not die; 5 for God knows
that when you eat of it your eyes will be opened, and you will be like God, knowing good and evil." 6 So when the
woman saw that the tree was good for food, and that it was a delight to the eyes, and that the tree was to be desired to
make one wise, she took of its fruit and ate; and she also gave some to her husband, who was with her, and he ate. 7
Then the eyes of both were opened, and they knew that they were naked; and they sewed fig leaves together and made
loincloths for themselves.

How I Met Your Mother

Musings

I'll get to the serpent in the next cartoon, but here I simply strayed from the story to imagine Adam and Eve's courtship just a bit. It shows just how lame the classic bar pick-up line really is. It didn't even impress Eve, even though Adam was the only guy on earth.

Back to the story, we see the crafty serpent working on Eve to eat the fruit. Even though a lot has been laid on Eve here, note that Adam just happened to be with her presumably for the whole time without saying anything. So they both get to share in the blame. Interestingly the things the serpent tells them are true and false at the same time. The fruit is good for eating, but it sort of kills them in the long run. It was good for knowledge, but it didn't make them like God. If anything they now lose their innocence and can make bad choices (as well as good) and become responsible for them. As animals, they were ignorant and amoral, now they are self-aware and can choose between bad and good and thus moral with the capacity to be immoral. While they had free will before the apple, now (because of their knowledge) they really are responsible for their decisions.

Genesis 3:8-19

Oopsy!

[8] They heard the sound of the LORD God walking in the garden at the time of the evening breeze, and the man and
his wife hid themselves from the presence of the LORD God among the trees of the garden. [9] But the LORD God called
to the man, and said to him, "Where are you?" [10] He said, "I heard the sound of you in the garden, and I was afraid,
because I was naked; and I hid myself." [11] He said, "Who told you that you were naked? Have you eaten from the tree
of which I commanded you not to eat?" [12] The man said, "The woman whom you gave to be with me, she gave me fruit
from the tree, and I ate." [13] Then the LORD God said to the woman, "What is this that you have done?" The woman
said, "The serpent tricked me, and I ate." [14] The LORD God said to the serpent, "Because you have done this, cursed are
you among all animals and among all wild creatures; upon your belly you shall go, and dust you shall eat all the days
of your life. [15] I will put enmity between you and the woman, and between your offspring and hers; he will strike your
head, and you will strike his heel." [16] To the woman he said, "I will greatly increase your pangs in childbearing; in pain
you shall bring forth children, yet your desire shall be for your husband, and he shall rule over you." [17] And to the man
he said, "Because you have listened to the voice of your wife, and have eaten of the tree about which I commanded
you, 'You shall not eat of it,' cursed is the ground because of you; in toil you shall eat of it all the days of your life; [18]
thorns and thistles it shall bring forth for you; and you shall eat the plants of the field. [19] By the sweat of your face you
shall eat bread until you return to the ground, for out of it you were taken; you are dust, and to dust you shall return."

The Blame Game

Musings

Here we get to the bad choices and consequences. God blames Adam, who blames Eve, who blames the serpent. The results are manifold. The serpent loses its arm and legs and must crawl on the ground forevermore. This explains snakes and ties the snake to the earth. It also could explain why women hate snakes. The woman gets pain in childbirth and subjugated to the man. Interesting. The man gets to work the soil, which will not be too fertile, for the rest of his life. This ties man back to the earth until he dies where he will return to dust. Remember it was from the dust he was created.

Genesis 3:20-24

Adam and Eve's Eviction Notice

[20] The man named his wife Eve, because she was the mother of all living. [21] And the LORD God made garments of
skins for the man and for his wife, and clothed them. [22] Then the LORD God said, "See, the man has become like one
of us, knowing good and evil; and now, he might reach out his hand and take also from the tree of life, and eat, and
live forever"-- [23] therefore the LORD God sent him forth from the garden of Eden, to till the ground from which he was
taken. [24] He drove out the man; and at the east of the garden of Eden he placed the cherubim, and a sword flaming and
turning to guard the way to the tree of life.

Key Master and Gate Keeper

Musings

Even though God kicks them out of the garden, God makes them clothes. That's kind of thoughtful really. God still loves them, even though they are bone heads. However, they still have to move out of the house (garden) and get a job. Worse, they can't go back. This actually seems like a metaphor to family life from just about any period in time. However it appears poor choices have cost Adam and Eve a very close relationship with God and a nice environment to live in. Some will suggest that this also introduces death into the equation, but I see nothing that indicates that they had eternal life to start with, because the tree of life in the garden is never really explained. So here is a story that can be viewed as humanities fall from grace (as well as for serpents) or as God still caring for and loving his creation even though they can't seem to use their new-found reason or knowledge all that well.

Genesis 6

Two Flood Stories Intertwined: Noah Finds Favor

9 These are the descendants of Noah. Noah was a righteous man, blameless in his generation; Noah walked with God. 10
And Noah had three sons, Shem, Ham, and Japheth. 11 Now the earth was corrupt in God's sight, and the earth was filled
with violence. 12 And God saw that the earth was corrupt; for all flesh had corrupted its ways upon the earth. 13 And God
said to Noah, "I have determined to make an end of all flesh, for the earth is filled with violence because of them; now
I am going to destroy them along with the earth. 14 Make yourself an ark of cypress wood; make rooms in the ark, and
cover it inside and out with pitch. 15 This is how you are to make it: the length of the ark three hundred cubits, its width
fifty cubits, and its height
thirty cubits. 16 Make a roof
for the ark, and finish it to
a cubit above; and put the
door of the ark in its side;
make it with lower, second,
and third decks. 17 For my
part, I am going to bring a
flood of waters on the earth,
to destroy from under heav-
en all flesh in which is the
breath of life; everything
that is on the earth shall
die. 18 But I will establish
my covenant with you; and
you shall come into the ark,
you, your sons, your wife,
and your sons' wives with
you. 19 And of every living
thing, of all flesh, you shall
bring two of every kind into
the ark, to keep them alive
with you; they shall be male
and female. 20 Of the birds
according to their kinds,
and of the animals accord-
ing to their kinds, of every
creeping thing of the ground
according to its kind, two of
every kind shall come in to
you, to keep them alive. 21 Also take with you every kind of food that is eaten, and store it up; and it shall serve as food
for you and for them." 22 Noah did this; he did all that God commanded him.

What Will the Neighbors Say

Musings

This cartoon is a tribute to Bill Cosby's brilliant comedy story of Noah's call from God to build an ark, with a nod to Morgan Freeman's movie portrayal of God in Bruce Almighty. Clearly Noah was called to do something quite extraordinary and neighbors as well as probably his own family thought he'd gone mad. Noah himself probably wondered as well, as the directions and shear size of an ark would be very hard to build. Granted God's "part" was much more difficult, but being God helps with the big stuff. No doubt Noah was overwhelmed. Of course Noah was selected for his righteousness, but one wonders if that was code for the only one that was crazy enough to do it.

Genesis 7

How Long Can You Tread Water?

*Then the LORD said to Noah, "Go into the ark, you and all your household, for I have seen that you alone are righ-
teous before me in this generation. 2 Take with you seven pairs of all clean animals, the male and its mate; and a pair
of the animals that are not clean, the male and its mate; 3 and seven pairs of the birds of the air also, male and female,
to keep their kind alive on the face of all the earth. 4 For in seven days I will send rain on the earth for forty days and
forty nights; and every living thing that I have made I will blot out from the face of the ground." 5 And Noah did all
that the LORD had commanded him. 6 Noah was six hundred years old when the flood of waters came on the earth. 7
And Noah with his sons and his wife and his sons' wives went into the ark to escape the waters of the flood. 8 Of clean
animals, and of animals that are not clean,
and of birds, and of everything that creeps on
the ground, 9 two and two, male and female,
went into the ark with Noah, as God had
commanded Noah. 10 And after seven days
the waters of the flood came on the earth. [...]
24 And the waters swelled on the earth for one
hundred fifty days.*

Have You Ever Seen Rain?

Musings

The two creation stories were preserved sequentially at the beginning of Genesis. Here there are actually two flood stories interwoven. The easiest sign of this is the discrepancy in the number of each kind of animal, seven pairs in one version and one pair in the other. There are other clues, but suffice it to say that one of the gems of the old testament is that it preserves more than just one point of view in many cases. Being oral tradition long before it was written down, it is amazing that they decided in some cases to keep complimentary stories (such as creation) and even different versions of the same story (flood). Rather than being in conflict, this often adds a richness to the texts that may have been lost otherwise. A new testament parallel would be if only one of the Gospels was included, much would be lost.

Notice we pick up Adam and Eve as marginal characters from here on out. It seems fitting that they should add their perspective to the events that followed. After all, they started it. In this case, I'd vote with Adam - based on clean-up and before that, boat size, I'd pick just a pair of each kind of animal.

Genesis 9

God's Rainbow Covenant

8 Then God said to Noah and to his sons with him, 9 "As for me, I am establishing my covenant with you and your descendants after you, 10 and with every living creature that is with you, the birds, the domestic animals, and every animal of the earth with you, as many as came out of the ark. 11 I establish my covenant with you, that never again shall all flesh be cut off by the waters of a flood, and never again shall there be a flood to destroy the earth." 12 God said, "This is the sign of the covenant that I make between me and you and every living creature that is with you, for all future generations: 13 I have set my bow in the clouds, and it shall be a sign of the covenant between me and the earth.
14 When I bring clouds over the earth and the bow is seen in the clouds, 15 I will remember my covenant that is between me and you and every living creature of all flesh; and the waters shall never again become a flood to destroy all flesh.
16 When the bow is in the clouds, I will see it and remember the everlasting covenant between God and every living creature of all flesh that is on the earth." 17 God said to Noah, "This is the sign of the covenant that I have established between me and all flesh that is on the earth."

God's Yellow Sticky Notes

Musings

Rounding out the flood story, God sets up a sign of the covenant with the people - the rainbow. This is a great way to take something occurring in nature and using it as a reminder about God. In the cartoon the rainbow seems to be there to remind God about the covenant, but it's doubtful God needs a reminder, but anything that gets people's minds back on God is a good symbol. This is even more fun since it appears in the sky (heavens), after a rain (flood), is awesome (like God) and on display for all the people to see. So the large, colorful sticky note is there for our benefit.

Genesis 11

The Tower of Babel

Now the whole earth had one language and the same words. 2 And as they migrated from the east, they came upon a plain in the land of Shinar and settled there. 3 And they said to one another, "Come, let us make bricks, and burn them thoroughly." And they had brick for stone, and bitumen for mortar. 4 Then they said, "Come, let us build ourselves a city, and a tower with its top in the heavens, and let us make a name for ourselves; otherwise we shall be scattered abroad upon the face of the whole earth." 5 The LORD came down to see the city and the tower, which mortals had built. 6 And the LORD said, "Look, they are one people, and they have all one language; and this is only the beginning of what they will do; nothing that they propose to do will now be impossible for them. 7 Come, let us go down, and confuse their language there, so that they will not understand one another's speech." 8 So the LORD scattered them abroad from there over the face of all the earth, and they left off building the city. 9 Therefore it was called Babel, because there the LORD confused the language of all the earth; and from there the LORD scattered them abroad over the face of all the earth.

There Goes the Neighborhood

Musings

How did all of the different nations and languages arise? Genesis, again, preserves two traditions attempting to explain it. First, in chapter 10, all the nations come from Noah's sons as they disburse across the land. A second account is given here with the story of Babel. Here "the whole earth" is still together. They attempt to preserve this unity by building a city and a very tall tower to make a name for themselves. This name or identity would keep them together. However, their plan is not God's plan. God confuses their language and scatters them abroad, and that's the end of their unity (or the beginning of their diversity). Notice the emphasis (underlines added) on the word "one" and "scattered" in this passage. Repetition is often a clue as to what is being stressed in the text.

In verse 7 God uses "us" while speaking about the mortals as is also done within the first creation story (1:26). In both cases most scholars think this is a use of the "royal we" (aka majestic plural) or an address to a heavenly court. It's hard to imagine that God feels threatened by people working and staying together, but whatever the reason, God doesn't allow it. Viva la difference!

Genesis 12

Abram the Ramblin' Man

Now the LORD said to Abram, "Go from your country and your kindred and your father's house to the land that I will show
you. 2 I will make of you a great nation, and I will bless you, and make your name great, so that you will be a blessing. 3 I will
bless those who bless you, and the one who curses you I will curse; and in you all the families of the earth shall be blessed." 4 So
Abram went, as the LORD had told him; and Lot went with him. Abram was seventy-five years old when he departed from
Haran. 5 Abram took his wife Sarai and his brother's son Lot, and all the possessions that they had gathered, and the persons
whom they had acquired in Haran; and they set forth to go to the land of Canaan. When they had come to the land of Canaan,
6 Abram passed through the land to the place at Shechem, to the oak of Moreh. At that time the Canaanites were in the land. 7
Then the LORD appeared to Abram, and said, "To your offspring I will give this land." So he built there an altar to the LORD,
who had appeared to him. 8 From there he moved on to the hill country on the east of Bethel, and pitched his tent, with Bethel
on the west and Ai on the east; and there he built an altar to the LORD and invoked the name of the LORD. 9 And Abram
journeyed on by stages toward the Negeb.

Perhaps They Asked Him to Leave?

Musings

This is the real beginning for the nation of Israel and the Hebrew people. It is God's covenant with Abram that begins the journey to nationhood and as a people. The main thing here is that Abram receive's God's call and in a tremendous act of faith (at 75 years old) sets out to the land of Canaan. God's promise to give all of the land to Abram and Sarai's offspring immediately sets up the story for some tension, as they don't have any children and are really too old to have any - or so they thought.

Genesis 15

God's Unilateral Covenant with Abe

*After these things the word of the LORD came to Abram in a vision, "Do not be afraid, Abram, I am your shield; your
reward shall be very great." 2 But Abram said, "O Lord GOD, what will you give me, for I continue childless, and the heir
of my house is Eliezer of Damascus?" 3 And Abram said, "You have given me no offspring, and so a slave born in my
house is to be my heir." 4 But the word of the LORD came to him, "This man shall not be your heir; no one but your very
own issue shall be your heir." 5 He brought him outside and said, "Look toward heaven and count the stars, if you are
able to count them." Then he said to him, "So shall your descendants be." 6 And he believed the LORD; and the LORD
reckoned it to him as righteousness. 7 Then he said to him, "I am the LORD who brought you from Ur of the Chaldeans,
to give you this land to possess." 8 But he said, "O Lord GOD, how am I to know that I shall possess it?" 9 He said to him,
"Bring me a heifer three years old, a female goat three years old, a ram three years old, a turtledove, and a young pi-
geon." 10 He brought him all these
and cut them in two, laying each
half over against the other; but
he did not cut the birds in two.
11 And when birds of prey came
down on the carcasses, Abram
drove them away. 12 As the sun
was going down, a deep sleep fell
upon Abram, and a deep and
terrifying darkness descended
upon him. [...] 17 When the sun
had gone down and it was dark,
a smoking fire pot and a flam-
ing torch passed between these
pieces. 18 On that day the LORD
made a covenant with Abram,
saying, "To your descendants I
give this land, from the river of
Egypt to the great river, the river
Euphrates [...]."*

Hey, At Least it's Not a Circumcision!

Musings

Here, again, is the first of two traditions regarding the covenant between God and Abram. In a traditional covenant, the animals are split in two and both parties walk in between the halves suggesting if either breaks the covenant, the fate of the animals would be their penalty as well. In this covenant, Abram falls asleep and only God walks between the halves. This shows it to be a unilateral covenant putting all the burden on God. That's pretty amazing when the more powerful party takes on the whole promise. There would normally be no incentive to do that.

Genesis 17

A Covenant that Hit's Below the Belt!

When Abram was ninety-nine years old, the LORD appeared to Abram, and said to him, "I am God Almighty; walk before me, and be blameless. 2 And I will make my covenant between me and you, and will make you exceedingly numerous." 3 Then Abram fell on his face; and God said to him, 4 "As for me, this is my covenant with you: You shall be the ancestor of a multitude of nations. 5 No longer shall your name be Abram, but your name shall be Abraham; for I have made you the ancestor of a multitude of nations. 6 I will make you exceedingly fruitful; and I will make nations of you, and kings shall come from you. 7 I will establish my covenant between me and you, and your offspring after you throughout their generations, for an everlasting covenant, to be God to you and to your offspring after you. 8 And I will give to you, and to your offspring after you, the land where you are now an alien, all the land of Canaan, for a perpetual holding; and I will be their God." 9 God said to Abraham, "As for you, you shall keep my covenant, you and your offspring after you throughout their generations. 10 This is my covenant, which you shall keep, between me and you and your offspring after you: Every male among you shall be circumcised. [...] 15 God said to Abraham, "As for Sarai your wife, you shall not call her Sarai, but Sarah shall be her name. 16 I will bless her, and moreover I will give you a son by her. I will bless her, and she shall give rise to nations; kings of peoples shall come from her." 17 Then Abraham fell on his face and laughed, and said to himself, "Can a child be born to a man who is a hundred years old? Can Sarah, who is ninety years old, bear a child?" 18 And Abraham said to God, "O that Ishmael might live in your sight!" 19 God said, "No, but your wife Sarah shall bear you a son, and you shall name him Isaac. I will establish my covenant with him as an everlasting covenant for his offspring after him.

Easy to Hide, Impossible to Deny

Musings

Here is the second story of the covenant. This promise emphasizes the promise of land and offspring, but there is an obligation on Abram's (or now Abraham's) part - circumcision. Circumcision is a very odd choice for a covenant, but it wasn't unique to Abraham's clan. It clearly requires a commitment on the part of adult males and, as the cartoon title suggests, it would be easy to hide but impossible to deny. I have to agree with cartoon Adam and Eve though.

The name play here is interesting as well. Abram or Abraham means "my father is exalted" or "father of a multitude," Sarai or Sarah means "princess" (as in mother of kings), and Isaac means "he laughs."

Genesis 22

The Father and Son Camp Out

After these things God tested Abraham. He said to him, "Abraham!" And he said, "Here I am." 2 He said, "Take your
son, your only son Isaac, whom you love, and go to the land of Moriah, and offer him there as a burnt offering on one
of the mountains that I shall show you." 3 So Abraham rose early in the morning, saddled his donkey, and took two of
his young men with him, and his son Isaac; he cut the wood for the burnt offering, and set out and went to the place
in the distance that God had shown him. 4 On the third day Abraham looked up and saw the place far away. 5 Then
Abraham said to his young men, "Stay here with the donkey; the boy and I will go over there; we will worship, and then
we will come back to you." 6 Abraham took the wood of the burnt offering and laid it on his son Isaac, and he himself
carried the fire and the knife. So the two of them walked on together. 7 Isaac said to his father Abraham, "Father!"
And he said, "Here I am, my son." He said, "The fire and the wood are here, but where is the lamb for a burnt offer-
ing?" 8 Abraham said, "God himself will provide the lamb for a burnt offering, my son." So the two of them walked on
together. 9 When they came to the place
that God had shown him, Abraham built
an altar there and laid the wood in or-
der. He bound his son Isaac, and laid him
on the altar, on top of the wood. 10 Then
Abraham reached out his hand and took
the knife to kill his son. 11 But the angel
of the LORD called to him from heaven,
and said, "Abraham, Abraham!" And he
said, "Here I am." 12 He said, "Do not lay
your hand on the boy or do anything to
him; for now I know that you fear God,
since you have not withheld your son,
your only son, from me." 13 And Abra-
ham looked up and saw a ram, caught
in a thicket by its horns. Abraham went
and took the ram and offered it up as a
burnt offering instead of his son. 14 So
Abraham called that place "The LORD
will provide"; as it is said to this day, "On
the mount of the LORD it shall be pro-
vided." 15 The angel of the LORD called to
Abraham a second time from heaven, 16
and said, "By myself I have sworn, says
the LORD: Because you have done this,
and have not withheld your son, your
only son, 17 I will indeed bless you, and I will make your offspring as numerous as the stars of heaven and as the sand
that is on the seashore. And your offspring shall possess the gate of their enemies, 18 and by your offspring shall all the
nations of the earth gain blessing for themselves, because you have obeyed my voice."

Ram Tough

Musings

In most English translations of the Bible "God" is used for various general words referring to God and "LORD" is reserved for when the original texts use "YHWH" or Yahweh, the most personal, special, holy name for the God the Abraham (or Israel). Here God (Elohim) tests Abraham's obedience with a horrible demand of human sacrifice, but the LORD (YHWH) stops him from going through with it. In fact the whole first half of the passage is God and the whole second half is LORD. Abraham passes the test and it seems clear the LORD is saying that human sacrifice is not to be done. This story is rich with other insights and ironies, but suffice it to say that there is no record of Isaac ever going camping with his Dad again.

Genesis 24
Isaac Gets a Wife

*[...]10 Then the servant took ten of his master's camels and departed, taking all kinds of choice gifts from his master;
and he set out and went to Aram-naharaim, to the city of Nahor. 11 He made the camels kneel down outside the city by
the well of water; it was toward evening, the time when women go out to draw water. 12 And he said, "O LORD, God of
my master Abraham, please grant me success today and show steadfast love to my master Abraham. 13 I am standing
here by the spring of water, and the daughters of the townspeople are coming out to draw water. 14 Let the girl to whom
I shall say, 'Please offer your jar that I may drink,' and who shall say, 'Drink, and I will water your camels'--let her be
the one whom you have appointed for your servant Isaac. By this I shall know that you have shown steadfast love to
my master." 15 Before he had finished speaking, there was Rebekah, who was born to Bethuel son of Milcah, the wife
of Nahor, Abraham's brother, coming out with her water jar on her shoulder. 16 The girl was very fair to look upon, a
virgin, whom no man had known. She went down to the spring, filled her jar, and came up. 17 Then the servant ran to
meet her and said, "Please let me sip
a little water from your jar." 18 "Drink,
my lord," she said, and quickly low-
ered her jar upon her hand and gave
him a drink. 19 When she had fin-
ished giving him a drink, she said, "I
will draw for your camels also, until
they have finished drinking." 20 So
she quickly emptied her jar into the
trough and ran again to the well to
draw, and she drew for all his camels.
21 The man gazed at her in silence to
learn whether or not the LORD had
made his journey successful. 22 When
the camels had finished drinking, the
man took a gold nose-ring weighing
a half shekel, and two bracelets for
her arms weighing ten gold shekels,
23 and said, "Tell me whose daughter
you are. Is there room in your father's
house for us to spend the night?" 24
She said to him, "I am the daughter
of Bethuel son of Milcah, whom she
bore to Nahor." [...] 29 Rebekah had
a brother whose name was Laban;
and Laban ran out to the man, to the
spring. 30 As soon as he had seen the
nose-ring, and the bracelets on his sister's arms, and when he heard the words of his sister Rebekah, "Thus the man
spoke to me," he went to the man; and there he was, standing by the camels at the spring. [...] 33 Then food was set before
him to eat; but he said, "I will not eat until I have told my errand." He said, "Speak on." 34 So he said, "I am Abraham's
servant. 35 The LORD has greatly blessed my master, and he has become wealthy; he has given him flocks and herds,
silver and gold, male and female slaves, camels and donkeys.*

How to Impress a Woman

Musings

This is a very odd way to pick out a wife for your son. A nose-ring? Really? Oh well (no pun intended).

Genesis 25

Esau and Jacob's Fun Loving Youth

*19 These are the descendants of Isaac, Abraham's son: Abraham was the father of Isaac, 20 and Isaac was forty years old
when he married Rebekah, daughter of Bethuel the Aramean of Paddan-aram, sister of Laban the Aramean. 21 Isaac
prayed to the LORD for his wife, because she was barren; and the LORD granted his prayer, and his wife Rebekah con-
ceived. 22 The children struggled together within her; and she said, "If it is to be this way, why do I live?" So she went to
inquire of the LORD. 23 And the LORD said to her, "Two nations are in your womb, and two peoples born of you shall
be divided; the one shall be stronger than the other, the elder shall serve the younger." 24 When her time to give birth was
at hand, there were twins in her womb. 25 The first came out red, all his body like a hairy mantle; so they named him
Esau. 26 Afterward his brother came out, with his hand gripping Esau's heel; so he was named Jacob. Isaac was sixty
years old when she bore them. 27 When the boys grew up, Esau was a skillful hunter, a man of the field, while Jacob was
a quiet man, living in tents. 28 Isaac loved Esau, because he was fond of game; but Rebekah loved Jacob. 29 Once when
Jacob was cooking a stew, Esau came in from the field, and he was famished. 30 Esau said to Jacob, "Let me eat some of
that red stuff, for I am famished!" (Therefore he was called Edom.) 31 Jacob said, "First sell me your birthright." 32 Esau
said, "I am about to die; of what use is a birthright to me?" 33 Jacob said, "Swear to me first." So he swore to him, and
sold his birthright to Jacob. 34 Then Jacob gave Esau bread and lentil stew, and he ate and drank, and rose and went his
way. Thus Esau despised his birthright.*

Is It Soup Yet?

Musings

Jacob is a sneaky little guy. Esau must have been incredibly hungry and not too bright. The first-born son gets a greater share of the family inheritance and the main blessing of the father. In this case Jacob cons Esau out of his birthright and later Rebekah and Jacob will con Isaac out of the blessing as well. The momma's boy wins.

Genesis 28

Jacob's 10% Solution (aka the Tithe)

10 Jacob left Beer-sheba and went toward Haran. 11 He came to a certain place and stayed there for the night, because the sun had set. Taking one of the stones of the place, he put it under his head and lay down in that place. 12 And he dreamed that there was a ladder set up on the earth, the top of it reaching to heaven; and the angels of God were ascending and descending on it. 13 And the LORD stood beside him and said, "I am the LORD, the God of Abraham your father and the God of Isaac; the land on which you lie I will give to you and to your offspring; 14 and your offspring shall be like the dust of the earth, and you shall spread abroad to the west and to the east and to the north and to the south; and all the families of the earth shall be blessed in you and in your offspring. 15 Know that I am with you and will keep you wherever you go, and will bring you back to this land; for I will not leave you until I have done what I have promised you." 16 Then Jacob woke from his sleep and said, "Surely the LORD is in this place--and I did not know it!" 17 And he was afraid, and said, "How awesome is this place! This is none other than the house of God, and this is the gate of heaven."

Jacob's Pillow!

Musings

Well Jacob's ladder gets all the glory, but Jacob's pillow is probably partly responsible for a bad night's sleep. It's a rock! It makes one wonder who was the first person to realize that even a wadded-up robe would be more comfortable. Oh and by-the-way, the covenant is re-stated by God for Jacob showing that God also recognizes that Jacob is the successor to Isaac. Of course, God knew that already, but that's beside the point.

Genesis 32

Jacob Gets a New Name - Israel

22 The same night he got up and took his two wives, his two maids, and his eleven children, and crossed the ford of the
Jabbok. 23 He took them and sent them across the stream, and likewise everything that he had. 24 Jacob was left alone;
and a man wrestled with him until daybreak. 25 When the man saw that he did not prevail against Jacob, he struck
him on the hip socket; and Jacob's hip was put out of joint as he wrestled with him. 26 Then he said, "Let me go, for the
day is breaking." But Jacob said, "I will not let you go, unless you bless me." 27 So he said to him, "What is your name?"
And he said, "Jacob." 28 Then the man said, "You shall no longer be called Jacob, but Israel, for you have striven with
God and with humans, and have prevailed." 29 Then Jacob asked him, "Please tell me your name." But he said, "Why is
it that you ask my name?" And there he blessed him. 30 So Jacob called the place Peniel, saying, "For I have seen God
face to face, and yet my life is preserved." 31 The sun rose upon him as he passed Penuel, limping because of his hip. 32
Therefore to this day the Israelites do not eat the thigh muscle that is on the hip socket, because he struck Jacob on the
hip socket at the thigh muscle.

Biblical Placement Ads

Musings

As we can see here, Jacob is really into getting blessed. It's interesting that Jacob, now called Israel, is afraid of Esau, but wrestled all night with God or an Angel of God. At the end the author throws in a little tidbit about a dietary practice resulting from Jacob's injury. A good excuse for not eating something that was probably pretty tough to begin with.

Genesis 37:1-11

Spoiled Brat Becomes a Rat

Jacob settled in the land where his father had lived as an alien, the land of Canaan. [2] This is the story of the family of Ja-
cob. Joseph, being seventeen years old, was shepherding the flock with his brothers; he was a helper to the sons of Bilhah
and Zilpah, his father's wives; and Joseph brought a bad report of them to their father. [3] Now Israel loved Joseph more
than any other of his children, because he was the son of his old age; and he had made him a long robe with sleeves. [4]
But when his brothers saw that their father loved him more than all his brothers, they hated him, and could not speak
peaceably to him. [5] Once Joseph had a dream, and when he told it to his brothers, they hated him even more. [6] He said
to them, "Listen to this dream that I dreamed. [7] There we were, binding sheaves in the field. Suddenly my sheaf rose
and stood upright; then your sheaves gathered around it, and bowed down to my sheaf." [8] His brothers said to him, "Are
you indeed to reign over us? Are you indeed to have dominion over us?" So they hated him even more because of his
dreams and his words. [9] He had another dream, and told it to his brothers, saying, "Look, I have had another dream:
the sun, the moon, and eleven stars were bowing down to me." [10] But when he told it to his father and to his brothers,
his father rebuked him, and said to him, "What kind of dream is this that you have had? Shall we indeed come, I and
your mother and your brothers, and bow to the ground before you?" [11] So his brothers were jealous of him, but his father kept the matter in mind.

I Know Something You Don't Know ...

Musings

The story of Joseph is one of the longest stories of any one person in Genesis. It spans almost 10 chapters or about 1/4th of Genesis. It is technically "the story of the family of Jacob," thus intended to be broader that just Joseph. In fact, it is very much concerned with the ethnic and tribal issues of Jacob's offspring even though Joseph maintains the central role. What is seldom mentioned about Joseph is that he was probably a spoiled brat. Jacob shows preference to Joseph, Joseph provides bad reports of his brothers, and then tells his two dreams to them. It is likely that two similar dreams and their repetition is to emphasize the brothers' hatred. Jealousy motivates them to try to keep Joseph's dream from coming true or, at least, it annoyed them greatly. Jacob seems to understands the dream and he is upset with Joseph for telling it to the brothers, although Jacob "kept the matter in mind."

An interesting side note here is that the story of Joseph is also the longest story about one person in the Koran, even though his legacy is not import to the genealogy of the Muslims. Comparing the two versions is fascinating, but for another time and book (such as (shameless plug) *Joseph: a Tale of Two Traditions*).

Genesis 37:12-36

Joseph's Lesson in Humility - Part 1 - Joseph's Brothers are the Pits!

12 Now his brothers went to pasture their father's flock near Shechem. 13 And Israel said to Joseph, "Are not your brothers pasturing the flock at
Shechem? Come, I will send you to them." He answered, "Here I am." 14 So he said to him, "Go now, see if it is well with your brothers and with
the flock; and bring word back to me." So he sent him from the valley of Hebron. He came to Shechem, 15 and a man found him wandering in
the fields; the man asked him, "What are you seeking?" 16 "I am seeking my brothers," he said; "tell me, please, where they are pasturing the
flock." 17 The man said, "They have gone away, for I heard them say, 'Let us go to Dothan.'" So Joseph went after his brothers, and found them at
Dothan. 18 They saw him from a distance, and before he came near to them, they conspired to kill him. 19 They said to one another, "Here comes
this dreamer. 20 Come now, let us kill him and throw him into one of the pits; then we shall say that a wild animal has devoured him, and we
shall see what will become of his dreams." 21 But when Reuben heard it, he delivered him out of their hands, saying, "Let us not take his life." 22
Reuben said to them, "Shed no blood; throw him into this pit here in the wilderness, but lay no hand on him"--that he might rescue him out of
their hand and restore him to his father. 23 So when Joseph came to his brothers, they stripped him of his robe, the long robe with sleeves that
he wore; 24 and they took him and threw him into a pit. The pit was empty; there was no water in it. 25 Then they sat down to eat; and looking
up they saw a caravan of Ishmaelites coming from Gilead, with their camels carrying gum, balm, and resin, on their way to carry it down
to Egypt. 26 Then Judah said to his brothers, "What profit is it if we kill our brother and conceal his blood? 27 Come, let us sell him to the Ish-
maelites, and not lay our hands on him, for he
is our brother, our own flesh." And his brothers
agreed. 28 When some Midianite traders passed
by, they drew Joseph up, lifting him out of the
pit, and sold him to the Ishmaelites for twenty
pieces of silver. And they took Joseph to Egypt. 29
When Reuben returned to the pit and saw that
Joseph was not in the pit, he tore his clothes.
30 He returned to his brothers, and said, "The
boy is gone; and I, where can I turn?" 31 Then
they took Joseph's robe, slaughtered a goat, and
dipped the robe in the blood. 32 They had the
long robe with sleeves taken to their father, and
they said, "This we have found; see now wheth-
er it is your son's robe or not." 33 He recognized
it, and said, "It is my son's robe! A wild animal
has devoured him; Joseph is without doubt torn
to pieces." 34 Then Jacob tore his garments, and
put sackcloth on his loins, and mourned for his
son many days. 35 All his sons and all his daugh-
ters sought to comfort him; but he refused to
be comforted, and said, "No, I shall go down
to Sheol to my son, mourning." Thus his father
bewailed him. 36 Meanwhile the Midianites had
sold him in Egypt to Potiphar, one of Pharaoh's
officials, the captain of the guard.

Tattle Tale Trap

Musings

Jacob sends Joseph to check on his brothers, who weren't where they should have been (another bad report for Joseph to file), so when they see him coming they plot to kill him. Then it is likely that there is a blending of two Jewish stories, Reuben the protector and Judah the protector. The result is the same, Joseph is sold to a caravan headed to Egypt (Midianites in the Reuben tradition and Ishmaelites in the Judah tradition). After Joseph is sold, the brothers put goat's blood on Joseph's shirt and take it to Jacob. Jacob, not the brothers, interprets the evidence and concludes that Joseph was "without a doubt" torn to pieces by wild animals. Then Jacob goes into extreme mourning over the death of the son of his favorite wife, Rachel (more so than when she died after giving birth to Benjamin, 35:20), and he cannot be consoled. So the brothers' jealousy causes them to act out of haste and then they must now live with the consequence of their actions. This also sets-up Jacob to be extra protective of Benjamin, as he is his youngest son and all that is left of Rachel's progeny (or so he believes).

Genesis 39

Joseph's Lesson in Humility - Part 2 - Potiphar's Wife

*Now Joseph was taken down to Egypt, and Potiphar, an officer of Pharaoh, the captain of the guard, an Egyptian, bought him
from the Ishmaelites who had brought him down there. 2 The LORD was with Joseph, and he became a successful man; he was
in the house of his Egyptian master. 3 His master saw that the LORD was with him, and that the LORD caused all that he did to
prosper in his hands. 4 So Joseph found favor in his sight and attended him; he made him overseer of his house and put him in
charge of all that he had. 5 From the time that he made him overseer in his house and over all that he had, the LORD blessed the
Egyptian's house for Joseph's sake; the blessing of the LORD was on all that he had, in house and field. 6 So he left all that he had
in Joseph's charge; and, with him there, he had no concern for anything but the food that he ate. Now Joseph was handsome and
good-looking. 7 And after a time his master's wife cast her eyes on Joseph and said, "Lie with me." 8 But he refused and said to his
master's wife, "Look, with me here, my master has no concern about anything in the house, and he has put everything that he has
in my hand. 9 He is not greater in this house than I am, nor has he kept back anything from me except yourself, because you are
his wife. How then could I do this great wickedness, and sin against God?" 10 And although she spoke to Joseph day after day, he
would not consent to lie beside her or to be with her. 11 One day, however, when he went into the house to do his work, and while
no one else was in the house, 12 she caught hold of his garment, saying, "Lie with me!" But he left his garment in her hand, and
fled and ran outside. 13 When she saw that
he had left his garment in her hand and had
fled outside, 14 she called out to the members
of her household and said to them, "See, my
husband has brought among us a Hebrew
to insult us! He came in to me to lie with
me, and I cried out with a loud voice; 15 and
when he heard me raise my voice and cry
out, he left his garment beside me, and fled
outside." 16 Then she kept his garment by her
until his master came home, 17 and she told
him the same story, saying, "The Hebrew
servant, whom you have brought among us,
came in to me to insult me; 18 but as soon
as I raised my voice and cried out, he left
his garment beside me, and fled outside." 19
When his master heard the words that his
wife spoke to him, saying, "This is the way
your servant treated me," he became en-
raged. 20 And Joseph's master took him and
put him into the prison, the place where the
king's prisoners were confined; he remained
there in prison. 21 But the LORD was with Jo-
seph and showed him steadfast love; he gave
him favor in the sight of the chief jailer. 22 The
chief jailer committed to Joseph's care all the
prisoners who were in the prison, and what-
ever was done there, he was the one who did
it. 23 The chief jailer paid no heed to anything
that was in Joseph's care, because the LORD
was with him; and whatever he did, the LORD made it prosper.*

She Who Laughs Last

Musings

One thing you can't miss from this passage is that the LORD was with Joseph and made everything he touched prosper. What is harder to see is that Joseph is still an arrogant spoiled brat. He flaunts success in the household in the face of Mrs. Potiphar, which is her domain. He has supplanted her. Whether she was drawn to him or just wanted him out of the house is debatable but she did succeed in getting him out of the house. Potiphar was no dummy though: what Joseph could do for his household, maybe he could do for his business. He was right, the LORD made Joseph's work prosper there as well.

Genesis 40

Lesson in Humility Part 3 - The Butcher, The Baker but no Candlestick Maker

*Some time after this, the cupbearer of the king of Egypt and his baker offended their lord the king of Egypt. 2 Pharaoh was angry
with his two officers, the chief cupbearer and the chief baker, 3 and he put them in custody in the house of the captain of the guard,
in the prison where Joseph was confined. 4 The captain of the guard charged Joseph with them, and he waited on them; and they
continued for some time in custody. 5 One night they both dreamed--the cupbearer and the baker of the king of Egypt, who were
confined in the prison--each his own dream, and each dream with its own meaning. 6 When Joseph came to them in the morn-
ing, he saw that they were troubled. 7 So he asked Pharaoh's officers, who were with him in custody in his master's house, "Why
are your faces downcast today?" 8 They said to him, "We have had dreams, and there is no one to interpret them." And Joseph
said to them, "Do not interpretations belong to God? Please tell them to me." 9 So the chief cupbearer told his dream to Joseph,
and said to him, "In my dream there was a vine before me, 10 and on the vine there were three branches. As soon as it budded,
its blossoms came out and the clusters ripened into grapes. 11 Pharaoh's cup was in my hand; and I took the grapes and pressed
them into Pharaoh's cup, and placed the cup in Pharaoh's hand." 12 Then Joseph said to him, "This is its interpretation: the three
branches are three days; 13 within three days Pharaoh will lift up your head and restore you to your office; and you shall place Pha-
raoh's cup in his hand, just as you used to do
when you were his cupbearer. 14 But remem-
ber me when it is well with you; please do
me the kindness to make mention of me to
Pharaoh, and so get me out of this place. 15
For in fact I was stolen out of the land of the
Hebrews; and here also I have done noth-
ing that they should have put me into the
dungeon." 16 When the chief baker saw that
the interpretation was favorable, he said to
Joseph, "I also had a dream: there were three
cake baskets on my head, 17 and in the up-
permost basket there were all sorts of baked
food for Pharaoh, but the birds were eating
it out of the basket on my head." 18 And Jo-
seph answered, "This is its interpretation:
the three baskets are three days; 19 within
three days Pharaoh will lift up your head--
from you!--and hang you on a pole; and the
birds will eat the flesh from you." 20 On the
third day, which was Pharaoh's birthday, he
made a feast for all his servants, and lifted
up the head of the chief cupbearer and the
head of the chief baker among his servants.
21 He restored the chief cupbearer to his cup-
bearing, and he placed the cup in Pharaoh's
hand; 22 but the chief baker he hanged, just
as Joseph had interpreted to them. 23 Yet the
chief cupbearer did not remember Joseph, but forgot him.*

I Have Some Good News and Some Bad News

Musings

In this installment, Joseph interprets two prisoners' dreams and asks one of them to remember him to Pharaoh, but he forgets. Joseph says that all interpretations belong to God (that God was with him was largely attested to in the prior passage). He not only asks the cupbearer to remember him to Pharaoh, but explains that he is only asking this because he was wronged twice, once by his own people (Hebrews) and once by false accusation from the Egyptians. His arrogance seems to be fading.

Genesis 41

Joseph, Joseph, He's Our Man, If He Can't Do It ...

*37 The proposal pleased Pharaoh and all his servants. 38 Pharaoh said to his servants, "Can we find anyone else like this--one in
whom is the spirit of God?" 39 So Pharaoh said to Joseph, "Since God has shown you all this, there is no one so discerning and wise
as you. 40 You shall be over my house, and all my people shall order themselves as you command; only with regard to the throne
will I be greater than you." 41 And Pharaoh said to Joseph, "See, I have set you over all the land of Egypt." 42 Removing his signet
ring from his hand, Pharaoh put it on Joseph's hand; he arrayed him in garments of fine linen, and put a gold chain around his
neck. 43 He had him ride in the chariot of his second-in-command; and they cried out in front of him, "Bow the knee!" Thus he set
him over all the land of Egypt. 44 Moreover Pharaoh said to Joseph, "I am Pharaoh, and without your consent no one shall lift up
hand or foot in all the land of Egypt." 45 Pharaoh gave Joseph the name Zaphenath-paneah; and he gave him Asenath daughter
of Potiphera, priest of On, as his wife. Thus Joseph gained authority over the land of Egypt. 46 Joseph was thirty years old when
he entered the service of Pharaoh king of Egypt. And Joseph went out from the presence of Pharaoh, and went through all the
land of Egypt. 47 During the seven plenteous years the earth produced abundantly. 48 He gathered up all the food of the seven years
when there was plenty in the land of Egypt,
and stored up food in the cities; he stored
up in every city the food from the fields
around it. 49 So Joseph stored up grain in
such abundance--like the sand of the sea--
that he stopped measuring it; it was beyond
measure. 50 Before the years of famine came,
Joseph had two sons, whom Asenath daugh-
ter of Potiphera, priest of On, bore to him.
51 Joseph named the firstborn Manasseh,
"For," he said, "God has made me forget all
my hardship and all my father's house." 52
The second he named Ephraim, "For God
has made me fruitful in the land of my mis-
fortunes." 53 The seven years of plenty that
prevailed in the land of Egypt came to an
end; 54 and the seven years of famine began
to come, just as Joseph had said. There was
famine in every country, but throughout the
land of Egypt there was bread. 55 When all
the land of Egypt was famished, the people
cried to Pharaoh for bread. Pharaoh said
to all the Egyptians, "Go to Joseph; what
he says to you, do." 56 And since the famine
had spread over all the land, Joseph opened
all the storehouses, and sold to the Egyp-
tians, for the famine was severe in the land
of Egypt. 57 Moreover, all the world came to
Joseph in Egypt to buy grain, because the
famine became severe throughout the world.*

The Right Man for the Job

Musings

Joseph is finally brought before Pharaoh and has a chance to again mention that it is God that brings the message, he is just the vehicle. Joseph has perhaps found some humility! This would appeal to a king, to think that God would be trying to give him a message. So in front of the whole court Joseph interprets the dreams. The significance of the two dreams is definitive (fixed by God or unchangeable). Then Joseph quite humbly lays out a plan of what the Pharaoh should do about the seven years of plenty and the seven years of famine: he must find a discerning and wise man to oversee the land (hint: Joseph)! The Pharaoh himself pronounces that Joseph is the wisest and most discerning in the land, acknowledging God in the process. He gives Joseph his signet ring, an Egyptian name (Zaphenath-paneah meaning "God Speaks" or "He Lives" or "Creator of Life") and a wife. Joseph's skills at administration are demonstrated and the famine has begun.

Genesis 42

Joseph Begins Messing with His Brothers!

When Jacob learned that there was grain in Egypt, he said to his sons, "Why do you keep looking at one another? 2 I have heard," he said, "that there is grain in Egypt; go down and buy grain for us there, that we may live and not die." 3 So ten of Joseph's brothers went down to buy grain in Egypt. 4 But Jacob did not send Joseph's brother Benjamin with his brothers, for he feared that harm might come to him. 5 Thus the sons of Israel were among the other people who came to buy grain, for the famine had reached the land of Canaan. 6 Now Joseph was governor over the land; it was he who sold to all the people of the land. And Joseph's brothers came and bowed themselves before him with their faces to the ground. 7 When Joseph saw his brothers, he recognized them, but he treated them like strangers and spoke harshly to them. "Where do you come from?" he said. They said, "From the land of Canaan, to buy food." 8 Although Joseph had recognized his brothers, they did not recognize him. 9 Joseph also remembered the dreams that he had dreamed about them. He said to them, "You are spies; you have come to see the nakedness of the land!" 10 They said to him, "No, my lord; your servants have come to buy food. 11 We are all sons of one man; we are honest men; your servants have never been spies." 12 But he said to them, "No, you have come to see the nakedness of the land!" 13 They said, "We, your servants, are twelve brothers, the sons of a certain man in the land of Canaan; the youngest, however, is now with our father, and one is no more." 14 But Joseph said to them, "It is just as I have said to you; you are spies! 15 Here is how you shall be tested: as Pharaoh lives, you shall not leave this place unless your youngest brother comes here! 16 Let one of you go and bring your brother, while the rest of you remain in prison, in order that your words may be tested, whether there is truth in you; or else, as Pharaoh lives, surely you are spies." 17 And he put them all together in prison for three days. 18 On the third day Joseph said to them, "Do this and you will live, for I fear God: 19 if you are honest men, let one of your brothers stay here where you are imprisoned. The rest of you shall go and carry grain for the famine of your households, 20 and bring your youngest brother to me. Thus your words will be verified, and you shall not die." And they agreed to do so. 21 They said to one another, "Alas, we are paying the penalty for what we did to our brother; we saw his anguish when he pleaded with us, but we would not listen. That is why this anguish has come upon us." 22 Then Reuben answered them, "Did I not tell you not to wrong the boy? But you would not listen. So now there comes a reckoning for his blood." 23 They did not know that Joseph understood them, since he spoke with them through an interpreter. 24 He turned away from them and wept; then he returned and spoke to them. And he picked out Simeon and had him bound before their eyes. 25 Joseph then gave orders to fill their bags with grain, to return every man's money to his sack, and to give them provisions for their journey. This was done for them.

Was I Dreaming or He's Not Heavy He's My Brother

Musings

Jacob is still in control of his family, and he sends the brothers to get grain. When Joseph sees them bow down before him, he remembers his dreams about the sheaves and the stars. He then takes the offensive: he accuses the brothers of being spies, devises a test and puts them all in jail. Later he releases all but Simeon and sends them back (with their money back in their sacks) on a mission to return with Benjamin if they want to prove their innocence. The brother's remember what they did to Joseph and Reuben scolds them. We also learn for the first time that Joseph pleaded with them, back at the pit, not to carry out their plan. Joseph overhears all of this discussion, so he has some feedback on how well his plan is going. The dreams' meaning becomes clear here: the stars and the moon dream point toward Joseph's status as royal vizier, and the sheaves to his role as provisioner. Joseph and the reader possibly get the first glimpse of the brothers' remorse. I believe it is also a fact that Joseph did use Groucho glasses - the perfect disguise.

Genesis 44

Joseph's Cup Runneth Over

*Then he commanded the steward of his house, "Fill the men's sacks with food, as much as they can carry, and put each man's
money in the top of his sack. 2 Put my cup, the silver cup, in the top of the sack of the youngest, with his money for the grain." And
he did as Joseph told him. 3 As soon as the morning was light, the men were sent away with their donkeys. 4 When they had gone
only a short distance from the city, Joseph said to his steward, "Go, follow after the men; and when you overtake them, say to
them, 'Why have you returned evil for good? Why have you stolen my silver cup? 5 Is it not from this that my lord drinks? Does he
not indeed use it for divination? You have done wrong in doing this.'" 6 When he overtook them, he repeated these words to them.
7 They said to him, "Why does my lord speak such words as these? Far be it from your servants that they should do such a thing!
8 Look, the money that we found at the top of our sacks, we brought back to you from the land of Canaan; why then would we
steal silver or gold from your lord's house? 9 Should it be found with any one of your servants, let him die; moreover the rest of us
will become my lord's slaves." 10 He said, "Even so; in accordance with your words, let it be: he with whom it is found shall become
my slave, but the rest of you shall go free."
11 Then each one quickly lowered his sack
to the ground, and each opened his sack. 12
He searched, beginning with the eldest and
ending with the youngest; and the cup was
found in Benjamin's sack. 13 At this they tore
their clothes. Then each one loaded his don-
key, and they returned to the city. 14 Judah
and his brothers came to Joseph's house while
he was still there; and they fell to the ground
before him. 15 Joseph said to them, "What
deed is this that you have done? Do you not
know that one such as I can practice divina-
tion?" 16 And Judah said, "What can we say
to my lord? What can we speak? How can we
clear ourselves? God has found out the guilt
of your servants; here we are then, my lord's
slaves, both we and also the one in whose
possession the cup has been found." 17 But he
said, "Far be it from me that I should do so!
Only the one in whose possession the cup was
found shall be my slave; but as for you, go up
in peace to your father."*

Between a Rock and a Hard Place

Musings

Here the story moves into dramatic high-gear. There is irony in identifying the stolen object as Joseph's divination cup. Joseph has twice denied that he divines at all (interpretation belongs to God alone), yet it is a plausible theft since he is the Pharaoh's vizier. The irony may simply be in the symbolism of Joseph's knowledge and the brothers' ignorance. However, there is a more important emphasis concerning Judah and his explanation of Jacob's perspective on the whole affair. In Judah's plea to take him instead of Benjamin, he provides a point-for-point undoing of the brothers' earlier wrongs. This is a true plea from the heart which even overlooks the unfairness of Jacob's preferential love of Benjamin and Joseph. It is possible that this is the climax of the story, since Judah's (and therefore the brothers') ignorance of their responsibility is lifted.

Genesis 45

Joseph Punks His Brothers

Then Joseph could no longer control himself before all those who stood by him, and he cried out, "Send everyone away
from me." So no one stayed with him when Joseph made himself known to his brothers. 2 And he wept so loudly that the
Egyptians heard it, and the household of Pharaoh heard it. 3 Joseph said to his brothers, "I am Joseph. Is my father still
alive?" But his brothers could not answer him, so dismayed were they at his presence. 4 Then Joseph said to his brothers,
"Come closer to me." And they came closer. He said, "I am your brother, Joseph, whom you sold into Egypt. 5 And now
do not be distressed, or angry with yourselves, because you sold me here; for God sent me before you to preserve life. 6
For the famine has been in the land these two years; and there are five more years in which there will be neither plow-
ing nor harvest. 7 God sent me before you to preserve for you a remnant on earth, and to keep alive for you many survi-
vors. 8 So it was not you who sent me here, but God; he has made me a father to Pharaoh, and lord of all his house and
ruler over all the land of Egypt. 9
Hurry and go up to my father and say to him, 'Thus says your son Joseph, God has made me lord of all Egypt; come down to me, do not
delay. 10 You shall settle in the land of Goshen, and you shall be near me, you and your children and your children's children, as well as your flocks, your herds, and
all that you have. 11 I will provide for you there--since there are five more years of famine to come--so that you and your household, and all that you have, will not come to poverty.'

Uh Oh! You've Been Had!

Musings

Judah's story causes Joseph to reveal his identity. The brothers have learned their lesson (although still not repentant). Joseph proceeds to enlighten them on the meaning of all that has happened to him, thus bringing them into an understanding of the truth. Basically it is time to go tell Jacob the good news and bring him to Egypt, so Joseph sent the brothers back with a regal caravan. It is possible that Joseph tells them not to argue on the way back, because they would likely have to explain their deed along with news that Joseph is alive (although the text does not provide it). So in a biblical sense, Joseph has just "punked" his brothers. It appears that he bears them no malice as, in a sense, it was as it had to be to fulfil God's original purpose and outlined in Joseph's dreams.

Genesis 46

Jacob Makes the Move

When Israel set out on his journey with all that he had and came to Beer-sheba, he offered sacrifices to the God of his father Isaac. [2] God spoke to Israel in visions of the night, and said, "Jacob, Jacob." And he said, "Here I am." [3] Then he said, "I am God, the God of your father; do not be afraid to go down to Egypt, for I will make of you a great nation there. [4] I myself will go down with you to Egypt, and I will also bring you up again; and Joseph's own hand shall close your eyes." [5] Then Jacob set out from Beer-sheba; and the sons of Israel carried their father Jacob, their little ones, and their wives, in the wagons that Pharaoh had sent to carry him. [6] They also took their livestock and the goods that they had acquired in the land of Canaan, and they came into Egypt, Jacob and all his offspring with him, [7] his sons, and his sons' sons with him, his daughters, and his sons' daughters; all his offspring he brought with him into Egypt. [8] Now these are the names of the Israelites, Jacob and his offspring, [...].

Say Cheese!

Musings

God speaks to Jacob at Beersheba to confirm that the move to Egypt is part of his plan, but also to foretell of their people's exodus to come. When God calls for Jacob (in his dream) he replies "Here I am," which is the same reply Joseph gives to Jacob at the beginning of the story when asked to go on a journey to check on his brothers. This is not the conclusion (after all this is the story of Jacob's family, not just Joseph), but it does provide a certain sense of closure to the main Joseph story line.

The Biblical account of course has more than what is selected here as its closing, because it is concluding not only the story of Jacob's family (the bulk of the text beyond chapter 45), but also the book of Genesis itself (to a lesser extent). Genesis begins with the creation of the universe and ends with the creation of the "chosen" race. The brothers do finally ask for forgiveness in an indirect sort of way, and it is clear that Joseph has forgiven them. Joseph's tribal legacy will live on through Ephraim and Manasseh (displacing Reuben) as the Bible story heads through the exodus and into Israel.

Exodus

Exodus 1

Joseph Forgotten and Israelites Oppressed

[6] Then Joseph died, and all his brothers, and that whole generation. [7] But the Israelites were fruitful and prolific; they
multiplied and grew exceedingly strong, so that the land was filled with them. [8] Now a new king arose over Egypt, who
did not know Joseph. [9] He said to his people, "Look, the Israelite people are more numerous and more powerful than
we. [10] Come, let us deal shrewdly with them, or they will increase and, in the event of war, join our enemies and fight
against us and escape from the land." [11] Therefore they set taskmasters over them to oppress them with forced labor.
They built supply cities, Pithom and Rameses, for Pharaoh. [12] But the more they were oppressed, the more they multi-
plied and spread, so that the Egyptians came to dread the Israelites. [13] The Egyptians became ruthless in imposing tasks
on the Israelites, [14] and made their lives bitter with hard service in mortar and brick and in every kind of field labor.
They were ruthless in all the tasks that they imposed on them.

Multiply and Divide

Musings

This sets the stage for the Israelites to leave Egypt for their own land. Joseph and all his wisdom and prosperity has been forgotten. Because of this, the Israelites are considered a threat and worse, they are multiplying like bunnies. The more the king tries to oppress them, the more prolific they become, and the more he oppresses them, and so on (like shampoo - rinse and repeat). We aren't told whether the Israelite people remember Joseph and the covenant of God with Abraham and Jacob, but it seems that they would since their 12 tribes are established under Jacob and play a part in the rest of the history of Israel's formation and kingdom.

Exodus 2:1-10

Steamboat Moses

Now a man from the house of Levi went and married a Levite woman. 2 The woman conceived and bore a son; and
when she saw that he was a fine baby, she hid him three months. 3 When she could hide him no longer she got a papy-
rus basket for him, and plastered it with bitumen and pitch; she put the child in it and placed it among the reeds on
the bank of the river. 4 His sister stood at a distance, to see what would happen to him. 5 The daughter of Pharaoh came
down to bathe at the river, while her attendants walked beside the river. She saw the basket among the reeds and sent
her maid to bring it. 6 When she opened it, she saw the child. He was crying, and she took pity on him, "This must be
one of the Hebrews' children," she said. 7 Then his sister said to Pharaoh's daughter, "Shall I go and get you a nurse from
the Hebrew women to nurse the child for you?" 8 Pharaoh's daughter said to her, "Yes." So the girl went and called the
child's mother. 9 Pharaoh's daughter said to her, "Take this child and nurse it for me, and I will give you your wages."
So the woman took the child and nursed it. 10 When the child grew up, she brought him to Pharaoh's daughter, and she
took him as her son. She named him Moses, "because," she said, "I drew him out of the water."

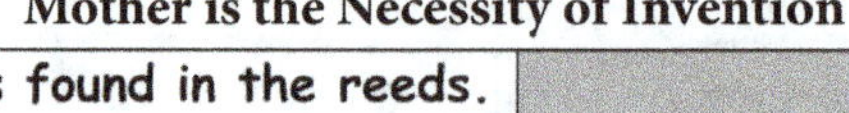

Mother is the Necessity of Invention

Musings

This is a pretty good gig for Moses' mother. She saves her son by setting him adrift to be discovered by Pharaoh's daughter, and then is actually paid to nurse (and probably raise) him. This story gives us a clever beginning, but is clearly not interested in Moses' childhood as can be gleaned from verse 9. The name Moses in Egyptian means "to be born" and in Hebrew might mean "to draw out." He is born to a Hebrew family, adopted son of Pharaoh's daughter, drawn out of the water and later draws his people out of Egypt. The name seems like a good fit.

Exodus 2:11-25

Moses Strikes Out on His Own

11 One day, after Moses had grown up, he went out to his people and saw their forced labor. He saw an Egyptian beating
a Hebrew, one of his kinsfolk. 12 He looked this way and that, and seeing no one he killed the Egyptian and hid him in
the sand. 13 When he went out the next day, he saw two Hebrews fighting; and he said to the one who was in the wrong,
"Why do you strike your fellow Hebrew?" 14 He answered, "Who made you a ruler and judge over us? Do you mean
to kill me as you killed the Egyptian?" Then Moses was afraid and thought, "Surely the thing is known." 15 When Pha-
raoh heard of it, he sought to kill Moses. But Moses fled from Pharaoh. He settled in the land of Midian, and sat down

Meet the Press

by a well. 16 The priest of Mid-
ian had seven daughters. They
came to draw water, and filled
the troughs to water their father's
flock. 17 But some shepherds came
and drove them away. Moses got
up and came to their defense
and watered their flock. 18 When
they returned to their father Re-
uel, he said, "How is it that you
have come back so soon today?"
19 They said, "An Egyptian helped
us against the shepherds; he even
drew water for us and watered
the flock." 20 He said to his daugh-
ters, "Where is he? Why did you
leave the man? Invite him to
break bread." 21 Moses agreed to
stay with the man, and he gave
Moses his daughter Zipporah in
marriage. 22 She bore a son, and
he named him Gershom; for he
said, "I have been an alien resid-
ing in a foreign land." 23 After a
long time the king of Egypt died.
The Israelites groaned under their
slavery, and cried out. Out of the
slavery their cry for help rose up
to God. 24 God heard their groaning, and God remembered his covenant with Abraham, Isaac, and Jacob. 25 God looked
upon the Israelites, and God took notice of them.

Musings

Clearly there was no press conference per se. It is used here to show how quickly news of, the now young adult, Moses' failed first attempt to help his people spread quickly. It's not clear in the Greek or Hebrew if Moses' intent was to kill the Egyptian, the word used indicates a very forceful beating, but regardless that was the result. Some scholars postulate this is the real reason Moses would not be allowed into the promised land. Note also that Moses is apparently aware of his heritage, identifying the Hebrews as kinfolk. There is clearly irony in the challenge to Moses about "who made you judge and ruler over us" since later it will be God that does so, yet for now he is a murderer trying to break up a fight, thus seen as hypocritical. However to Reuel's (aka Jethro) daughters he is a bit of a hero. It is also clear that he does not like injustice wherever he sees it ... Egyptians, Hebrews or Midianites. All this is likely preparing him for what is to come. Moses is destined to always be considered somewhat of an outcast. Here in this short passage Moses goes from privileged to outcast to homeless to foreigner.

Exodus 3:1-12

One in the Burning Bush is Worth Two in the Hand

Moses was keeping the flock of his father-in-law Jethro, the priest of Midian; he led his flock beyond the wilderness, and
came to Horeb, the mountain of God. 2 There the angel of the LORD appeared to him in a flame of fire out of a bush;
he looked, and the bush was blazing, yet it was not consumed. 3 Then Moses said, "I must turn aside and look at this
great sight, and see why the bush is not burned up." 4 When the LORD saw that he had turned aside to see, God called
to him out of the bush, "Moses, Moses!" And he said, "Here I am." 5 Then he said, "Come no closer! Remove the sandals
from your feet, for the place on which you are standing is holy ground." 6 He said further, "I am the God of your father,
the God of Abraham, the God of Isaac, and the God of Jacob." And Moses hid his face, for he was afraid to look at
God. 7 Then the LORD said, "I have observed the misery of my people who are in Egypt; I have heard their cry on ac-
count of their taskmasters. Indeed, I know their sufferings, 8 and I have come down to deliver them from the Egyptians,
and to bring them up out of that land to
a good and broad land, a land flowing
with milk and honey, to the country of
the Canaanites, the Hittites, the Amori-
tes, the Perizzites, the Hivites, and the
Jebusites. 9 The cry of the Israelites has
now come to me; I have also seen how
the Egyptians oppress them. 10 So come,
I will send you to Pharaoh to bring my
people, the Israelites, out of Egypt." 11
But Moses said to God, "Who am I that
I should go to Pharaoh, and bring the
Israelites out of Egypt?" 12 He said, "I
will be with you; and this shall be the
sign for you that it is I who sent you:
when you have brought the people out
of Egypt, you shall worship God on this
mountain."

What's in the Name?

What's in the Name?

13 But Moses said to God, "If I come to
the Israelites and say to them, 'The God
of your ancestors has sent me to you,'
and they ask me, 'What is his name?'
what shall I say to them?" 14 God said to
Moses, "I AM WHO I AM." He said fur-
ther, "Thus you shall say to the Israelites,
'I AM has sent me to you.'" 15 God also said to Moses, "Thus you shall say to the Israelites, 'The LORD, the God of your
ancestors, the God of Abraham, the God of Isaac, and the God of Jacob, has sent me to you': This is my name forever,
and this my title for all generations.

Musings

Moses at the burning bush is perhaps one of the funniest scenes in the Old Testament. It was a widely held belief that knowing a deity's true name gave power over it (to invoke the deity to do one's own bidding). Moses wasn't necessarily going for that, but contrary to his excuse (the Israelites will need convincing) it was he who needed the reassurance (Moses never uses the "I AM" with the Israelites). God's answer was essentially "none of your business" ("I am that I am" or "I am what I will be"). YHWH (LORD) and God (Elohim) was good enough for the Hebrews and it was going to be good enough for Moses, and apparently it was after this discussion. Humor aside, there is not doubt that there is a sincere and complex struggle going on within Moses as he tries to come to grips with this mission. Moses' struggles aside, the mission itself is a very positive message: God is responding out of love to deliver the Hebrews from their affliction.

Exodus 3:13-20
The Plan
16 Go and assemble the elders of Israel, and say to them, 'The LORD, the God of your ancestors, the God of Abraham, of
Isaac, and of Jacob, has appeared to me, saying: I have given heed to you and to what has been done to you in Egypt.
17 I declare that I will bring you up out of the misery of Egypt, to the land of the Canaanites, the Hittites, the Amorites,
the Perizzites, the Hivites, and the Jebusites, a land flowing with milk and honey.' 18 They will listen to your voice; and
you and the elders of Israel shall go to the king of Egypt and say to him, 'The LORD, the God of the Hebrews, has met
with us; let us now go a three days' journey into the wilderness, so that we may sacrifice to the LORD our God.' 19 I
know, however, that the king of Egypt will not let you go unless compelled by a mighty hand. 20 So I will stretch out
my hand and strike Egypt with all my wonders that I will perform in it; after that he will let you go. 21 I will bring this
people into such favor with the Egyptians that, when you go, you will not go empty-handed; 22 each woman shall ask
her neighbor and any woman living in the neighbor's house for jewelry of silver and of gold, and clothing, and you shall
put them on your sons and on your daughters; and so you shall plunder the Egyptians."

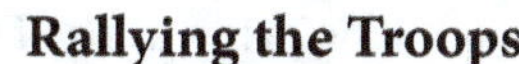

Rallying the Troops

Musings
The negotiations between Moses and God (as if you can negotiate with God) continue up through verse 4:18 (the lectionary stops at 3:20). God counters every excuse that Moses comes up with, including simply asking God to send someone else. God actually becomes angry, but Moses ends up going along with the plan and gets his brother Aaron as a spokes-person. This cartoon simply shows what may have been playing out in Moses' head as to how the "plan" would be received. It's understandable why he wasn't too confident about it.

Exodus 12

The Passover

The LORD said to Moses and Aaron in the land of Egypt: 2 This month shall mark for you the beginning of months; it shall be the first month of the year for you. 3 Tell the whole congregation of Israel that on the tenth of this month they are to take a lamb for each family, a lamb for each household. 4 If a household is too small for a whole lamb, it shall join its closest neighbor in obtaining one; the lamb shall be divided in proportion to the number of people who eat of it. 5 Your lamb shall be without blemish, a year-old male; you may take it from the sheep or from the goats. 6 You shall keep it until the fourteenth day of this month; then the whole assembled congregation of Israel shall slaughter it at twilight. 7 They shall take some of the blood and put it on the two doorposts and the lintel of the houses in which they eat it. 8 They shall eat the lamb that same night; they shall eat it roasted over the fire with unleavened bread and bitter herbs. 9 Do not eat any of it raw or boiled in water, but roasted over the fire, with its head, legs, and inner organs. 10 You shall let none of it remain until the morning; anything that remains until the morning you shall burn. 11 This is how you shall eat it: your loins girded, your sandals on your feet, and your staff in your hand; and you shall eat it hurriedly. It is the passover of the LORD. 12 For I will pass through the land of Egypt that night, and I will strike down every firstborn in the land of Egypt, both human beings and animals; on all the gods of Egypt I will execute judgments: I am the LORD.

Someone's Knocking at the Door

13 The blood shall be a sign for you on the houses where you live: when I see the blood, I will pass over you, and no plague shall destroy you when I strike the land of Egypt. 14 This day shall be a day of remembrance for you. You shall celebrate it as a festival to the LORD; throughout your generations you shall observe it as a perpetual ordinance.

Musings

The story takes a bit of a break between the 9th and 10th (final) plagues to provide the details of the Festival of the Passover and Unleaven Bread. The festival of the unleaven bread was probably originally a separate festival celebrating the barley harvest, but it fits well the passover. So it is that the passover commemorates the saving of their firstborn, or the passing over of the LORD, and the unleaven bread commemorates the exodus from slavery to their own land. It is likely that the Pharaoh, while disappointed he lost all his slave labor was pretty happy about not having to talk to Moses and Aaron any more.

Exodus 14
No Lifeguard on Duty

[19] The angel of God who was going before the Israelite army moved and went behind them; and the pillar of cloud moved
from in front of them and took its place behind them. [20] It came between the army of Egypt and the army of Israel. And
so the cloud was there with the darkness, and it lit up the night; one did not come near the other all night. [21] Then Moses
stretched out his hand over the sea. The LORD drove the sea back by a strong east wind all night, and turned the sea
into dry land; and the waters were divided. [22] The Israelites went into the sea on dry ground, the waters forming a wall
for them on their right and on their left. [23] The Egyptians pursued, and went into the sea after them, all of Pharaoh's
horses, chariots, and chariot drivers. [24] At the morning watch the LORD in the pillar of fire and cloud looked down

Taking the Short Cut

upon the Egyptian army, and
threw the Egyptian army into
panic. [25] He clogged their chariot
wheels so that they turned with
difficulty. The Egyptians said,
"Let us flee from the Israelites,
for the LORD is fighting for them
against Egypt." [26] Then the LORD
said to Moses, "Stretch out your
hand over the sea, so that the
water may come back upon the
Egyptians, upon their chariots
and chariot drivers." [27] So Mo-
ses stretched out his hand over
the sea, and at dawn the sea re-
turned to its normal depth. As
the Egyptians fled before it, the
LORD tossed the Egyptians into
the sea. [28] The waters returned
and covered the chariots and the
chariot drivers, the entire army of
Pharaoh that had followed them
into the sea; not one of them
remained. [29] But the Israelites
walked on dry ground through
the sea, the waters forming a
wall for them on their right and
on their left. [30] Thus the LORD
saved Israel that day from the
Egyptians; and Israel saw the Egyptians dead on the seashore. [31] Israel saw the great work that the LORD did against
the Egyptians. So the people feared the LORD and believed in the LORD and in his servant Moses.

Musings

This may one of the three best known scenes in the Old Testament, right up there with Adam and Eve in the Garden and Noah's Ark. Perhaps due in large part to Cecil B. De Mille's epic film, The Ten Commandments, starring Charlton Heston as Moses. In fact, it's very hard to even cartoon Moses without it being somewhat of caricature of Heston! This is the biblical equivalent of a chase scene in modern movies, only the "chase" took a fair bit of time and some divine intervention assisting the good guys.

From a narrative point of view, the exodus begins with God parting the Reed (or Red) Sea and ends with God parting the waters of the Jordan for entry into the promised land.

Exodus 16

The Journey Begins

The whole congregation of the Israelites set out from Elim; and Israel came to the wilderness of Sin, which is between
Elim and Sinai, on the fifteenth day of the second month after they had departed from the land of Egypt. 2 The whole
congregation of the Israelites complained against Moses and Aaron in the wilderness. 3 The Israelites said to them, "If
only we had died by the hand of the LORD in the land of Egypt, when we sat by the fleshpots and ate our fill of bread; for
you have brought us out into this wilderness to kill this whole assembly with hunger." 4 Then the LORD said to Moses,
"I am going to rain bread from heaven for you, and each day the people shall go out and gather enough for that day. In
that way I will test them, whether they will follow my instruction or not. 5 On the sixth day, when they prepare what they
bring in, it will be twice as much as they gather on other days." 6 So Moses and Aaron said to all the Israelites, "In the
evening you shall know that it was the LORD who brought you out of the land of Egypt, 7 and in the morning you shall
see the glory of the LORD, because he has heard your complaining against the LORD. For what are we, that you com-
plain against us?" 8 And
Moses said, "When the
LORD gives you meat to
eat in the evening and
your fill of bread in the
morning, because the
LORD has heard the
complaining that you ut-
ter against him--what are
we? Your complaining is
not against us but against
the LORD." 9 Then Moses
said to Aaron, "Say to the
whole congregation of
the Israelites, 'Draw near
to the LORD, for he has
heard your complaining.'"
10 And as Aaron spoke
to the whole congrega-
tion of the Israelites, they
looked toward the wil-
derness, and the glory of
the LORD appeared in
the cloud. 11 The LORD
spoke to Moses and said,

Are We There Yet?!

12 "I have heard the complaining of the Israelites; say to them, 'At twilight you shall eat meat, and in the morning you
shall have your fill of bread; then you shall know that I am the LORD your God.'" 13 In the evening quails came up and
covered the camp; and in the morning there was a layer of dew around the camp. 14 When the layer of dew lifted, there
on the surface of the wilderness was a fine flaky substance, as fine as frost on the ground. 15 When the Israelites saw
it, they said to one another, "What is it?" For they did not know what it was. Moses said to them, "It is the bread that
the LORD has given you to eat.

Musings

Well, the whining and complaining is probably to be expected of a large group that really just doesn't seem to get the big picture. It's not like they didn't witness the parting of the sea, 10 plagues and all of that, but the past is quickly forgotten when the present seems so miserable. However, they get a quail at night and bread in the mornings. Not exactly a bed and breakfast, but clearly they aren't starving either. Fortunately God is looking out for them. Unfortunately they seem to complain quickly and not follow directions all that well (if you read on into subsequent verses where they fail the test about keeping leftovers and gather for the Sabbath).

Exodus 17

Moses the Civil Engineer

From the wilderness of Sin the whole congregation of the Israelites journeyed by stages, as the LORD commanded. They camped at Rephidim, but there was no water for the people to drink. [2] *The people quarreled with Moses, and said, "Give us water to drink." Moses said to them, "Why do you quarrel with me? Why do you test the LORD?"* [3] *But the people thirsted there for water; and the people complained against Moses and said, "Why did you bring us out of Egypt, to kill us and our children and livestock with thirst?"* [4] *So Moses cried out to the LORD, "What shall I do with this people? They are almost ready to stone me."* [5] *The LORD said to Moses, "Go on ahead of the people, and take some of the elders of Israel with you; take in your hand the staff with which you struck the Nile, and go.* [6] *I will be standing there in front of you on the rock at Horeb. Strike the rock, and water will come out of it, so that the people may drink." Moses did so, in the sight of the elders of Israel.* [7] *He called the place Massah and Meribah, because the Israelites quarreled and tested the LORD, saying, "Is the LORD among us or not?"*

The First Tap Water

Musings

Names of places are often a clue to what has or will happen there. Rephidim means refresh or support and in this story it leads to refreshment and later support in war. Massah and Meribah mean trial and quarrel respectively and is also fitting. The type of quarrel they bring to Moses is more like a law suit challenging Moses (or God) to prove that God is with them. To this point God is testing the Israelites, but this is a bit of a push-back. So, God shows that God is with them by being present at the rock (a rock is symbolic of strength or might and permanence) and providing the water they have requested as proof. God probably regrets the whole free will thing here as in many other places in the Bible.

Exodus 19

On Top of Old Smokey

16 On the morning of the third day there was thunder and lightning, as well as a thick cloud on the mountain, and a
blast of a trumpet so loud that all the people who were in the camp trembled. 17 Moses brought the people out of the
camp to meet God. They took their stand at the foot of the mountain. 18 Now Mount Sinai was wrapped in smoke, be-
cause the LORD had descended upon it in fire; the smoke went up like the smoke of a kiln, while the whole mountain
shook violently. 19 As the blast of the trumpet grew louder and louder, Moses would speak and God would answer him
in thunder. 20 When the LORD descended upon Mount Sinai, to the top of the mountain, the LORD summoned Moses
to the top of the mountain, and Moses went up. 21 Then the LORD said to Moses, "Go down and warn the people not
to break through to the LORD to look; otherwise many of them will perish. 22 Even the priests who approach the LORD
must consecrate themselves or the LORD will break out against them." 23 Moses said to the LORD, "The people are not
permitted to come up to Mount Sinai; for you yourself warned us, saying, 'Set limits around the mountain and keep it
holy.'" 24 The LORD said to him, "Go down, and come up bringing Aaron with you; but do not let either the priests or
the people break through to come up to the LORD; otherwise he will break out against them."

Who Loves You?

Musings

Very little press seems to be given to this passage, but it is where the Israelites meet God pretty much up close and personal. It's not a private theophany like the appearance of God to Moses was at the burning bush, it is a full-out appearance to the entire group. It is believed the subject of discussion in verse 19 is none other than the 10 commandments, later put on tablets (twice) and kept in a place of honor (believed to be the contents of the Ark of the Covenant).

The Ten Commandments deserve their own commentary because there is just so much in them, so in the second and last shameless plug in this book, refer to the commentary *The Cartoon Ten Commandments*, for an in-depth look at them! History shows the Israelites were good caretakers of these rules, because these concepts have become the basis for most laws and legal systems throughout the world today.

Exodus 20

Hang Ten

*Then God spoke all these words: [2] I am the LORD your God, who brought you out of the land of Egypt, out of the house of slavery; [3] you shall
have no other gods before me. [4] You shall not make for yourself an idol, whether in the form of anything that is in heaven above, or that is
on the earth beneath, or that is in the water under the earth. [5] You shall not bow down to them or worship them; for I the LORD your God
am a jealous God, punishing children for the iniquity of parents, to the third and the fourth generation of those who reject me, [6] but showing
steadfast love to the thousandth generation of those who love me and keep my commandments. [7] You shall not make wrongful use of the name
of the LORD your God, for the LORD will not acquit anyone who misuses his name. [8] Remember the sabbath day, and keep it holy. [9] Six days
you shall labor and do all your work. [10] But the seventh day is a sabbath to the LORD your God; you shall not do any work--you, your son or
your daughter, your male or female slave, your livestock, or the alien resident in your towns. [11] For in six days the LORD made heaven and
earth, the sea, and all that is in them, but rested the seventh day; therefore the LORD blessed the sabbath day and consecrated it. [12] Honor
your father and your mother, so that your days may be long in the land that the LORD your God is giving you. [13] You shall not murder. [14] You
shall not commit adultery. [15] You shall not steal. [16] You shall not bear false witness against your neighbor. [17] You shall not covet your neighbor's
house; you shall not covet your neighbor's wife, or male or female slave, or ox, or donkey, or anything that belongs to your neighbor. [18] When
all the people witnessed the thunder and lightning, the sound of the trumpet, and the mountain smoking, they were afraid and trembled and
stood at a distance, [19] and said to Moses, "You speak to us, and we will listen; but do not let God speak to us, or we will die." [20] Moses said to
the people, "Do not be afraid; for God has come only to test you and to put the fear of him upon you so that you do not sin." [21] Then the people
stood at a distance, while Moses drew near to the thick darkness where God was.*

Moses and Aaron Discuss the Fine Print

Musings

The Israelite people have just fled from Egypt where they had been slaves for 400 years. Now they are free and looking for the promised land of their own, yet alone in the desert not really knowing where they are headed. It is at this time God gives the Israelites the Ten Commandments. What made the Israelites a nation even before they had a land of their own was their belief in one God and the way they were to live.

How would it feel to hear God speak directly? Awesome, amazing, frightening, special, dangerous? It is hard to imagine, but it does help to understand why Moses and the Israelite people felt that the Ten Commandments were very important indeed. It also isn't hard to understand their request in verse 19 - they will let Moses do the talking to God!

Exodus 24
Mountain Climbing with God

9 Then Moses and Aaron, Nadab, and Abihu, and seventy of the elders of Israel went up, 10 and they saw the God of
Israel. Under his feet there was something like a pavement of sapphire stone, like the very heaven for clearness. 11 God
did not lay his hand on the chief men of the people of Israel; also they beheld God, and they ate and drank. 12 The LORD
said to Moses, "Come up to me on the mountain, and wait there; and I will give you the tablets of stone, with the law
and the commandment, which I have written for their instruction." 13 So Moses set out with his assistant Joshua, and
Moses went up into the mountain of God. 14 To the elders he had said, "Wait here for us, until we come to you again;
for Aaron and Hur are with you; whoever has a dispute may go to them." 15 Then Moses went up on the mountain,
and the cloud covered the mountain. 16 The glory of the LORD settled on Mount Sinai, and the cloud covered it for six
days; on the seventh day he called to Moses out of the cloud. 17 Now the appearance of the glory of the LORD was like
a devouring fire on the top of the mountain in the sight of the people of Israel. 18 Moses entered the cloud, and went up
on the mountain. Moses was on the mountain for forty days and forty nights.

Take 2 Tablets and Call Me in the Morning

Musings

This begins the story of the first set of tablets. The first part of the passage (verses 9-11) seems unusual in that one big priestly group of Israel had a rather casual meeting with God (in that they saw God and didn't die), Moses isn't singled out, and they ate and drank affirming the covenant. It is possible this is preserved from a different tradition. Soon it is more like the rest of the story with Moses and now Joshua having a special audience with God and working on the tablets recording the commandments. Meanwhile the rest of the Israelites are at the base of the mountain now under the care of Aaron and the priests. What could go wrong?

Exodus 32
The Golden Calf

*When the people saw that Moses delayed to come down from the mountain, the people gathered around Aaron, and
said to him, "Come, make gods for us, who shall go before us; as for this Moses, the man who brought us up out of the
land of Egypt, we do not know what has become of him." 2 Aaron said to them, "Take off the gold rings that are on the
ears of your wives, your sons, and your daughters, and bring them to me." 3 So all the people took off the gold rings from
their ears, and brought them to Aaron. 4 He took the gold from them, formed it in a mold, and cast an image of a calf;
and they said, "These are your gods, O Israel, who brought you up out of the land of Egypt!" 5 When Aaron saw this, he
built an altar before it; and Aaron made proclamation and said, "Tomorrow shall be a festival to the LORD." 6 They rose
early the next day, and offered burnt offerings and brought sacrifices of well-being; and the people sat down to eat and
drink, and rose up to revel. 7 The LORD said to Moses, "Go down at once! Your people, whom you brought up out of the
land of Egypt, have acted perversely; 8 they have been quick to turn aside from the way that I commanded them; they
have cast for themselves an image of a calf, and have worshiped it and sacrificed to it, and said, 'These are your gods,
O Israel, who brought you up out of the land
of Egypt!'" 9 The LORD
said to Moses, "I have seen this people, how
stiff-necked they are. 10
Now let me alone, so that my wrath may burn hot against them and I may consume them; and of you I will make a
great nation." 11 But Moses implored the LORD his God, and said, "O LORD, why does your wrath burn hot against your people, whom you brought out of the land of Egypt with great power and with a mighty
hand? 12 Why should the Egyptians say, 'It was with evil intent that he brought them out to kill them in the mountains,
and to consume them from the face of the earth'? Turn from your fierce wrath; change your mind and do not bring
disaster on your people. 13 Remember Abraham, Isaac, and Israel, your servants, how you swore to them by your own
self, saying to them, 'I will multiply your descendants like the stars of heaven, and all this land that I have promised I
will give to your descendants, and they shall inherit it forever.'" 14 And the LORD changed his mind about the disaster
that he planned to bring on his people.*

God Give Me Patience NOW!

Musings

If the people were worried about why Moses was delayed you would think they'd organize a search party, instead they sought to replace him as a messenger of God with a golden calf. Some see this as idolatry but some think that the golden calf was not going to be worshipped as a god, but rather as a pedestal or intermediary in Moses' absence. Maybe it was just a good excuse to have an orgy (the work translated as "revel" has sexual connotations). Interestingly God tells Moses to go down at once to your people (as opposed to "my" people). God is pretty annoyed at them and while Moses talks God out of simply wiping them out, there will be consequences.

Exodus 33

Moses Sees God - Sort Of

[12] Moses said to the LORD, "See, you have said to me, 'Bring up this people'; but you have not let me know whom you will send with me. Yet you have said, 'I know you by name, and you have also found favor in my sight.' [13] Now if I have found favor in your sight, show me your ways, so that I may know you and find favor in your sight. Consider too that this nation is your people." [14] He said, "My presence will go with you, and I will give you rest." [15] And he said to him, "If your presence will not go, do not carry us up from here. [16] For how shall it be known that I have found favor in your sight, I and your people, unless you go with us? In this way, we shall be distinct, I and your people, from every people on the face of the earth." [17] The LORD said to Moses, "I will do the very thing that you have asked; for you have found favor in my sight, and I know you by name." [18] Moses said, "Show me your glory, I pray." [19] And he said, "I will make all my goodness pass before you, and will proclaim before you the name, 'The LORD'; and I will be gracious to whom I will be gracious, and will show mercy on whom I will show mercy. [20] But," he said, "you cannot see my face; for no one shall see me and live." [21] And the LORD continued, "See, there is a place by me where you shall stand on the rock; [22] and while my glory passes by I will put you in a cleft of the rock, and I will cover you with my hand until I have passed by; [23] then I will take away my hand, and you shall see my back; but my face shall not be seen."

23 Skiddoo

Musings

Here is Moses working on God to give him more insight into who YHWH is, similar to his exchange back at the burning bush. Here God grants Moses everything he asks for except, again, any further insight into his name. Instead of I AM (what I will be), he lets Moses know that God will be gracious to whom and when God wants. The name YHWH will have to do. Also, God will pass by but Moses will not see God's face, only God's back. This may mean that God's existence and nature will be make known by God's actions and deeds. God's presence will be with Moses and his people, but God will also remain mysterious.

In addition to the closer relationship Moses is having with the LORD, he successfully intercedes on the behalf of the Israelites. Essentially God wasn't going with them in the wilderness after the golden calf incident, but agrees to do so again. God shows mercy and grace and is willing to start over.

Exodus 34

The First Tanning Booth

29 Moses came down from Mount Sinai. As he came down from the mountain with the two tablets of the covenant in his hand, Moses did not know that the skin of his face shone because he had been talking with God.
30 When Aaron and all the Israelites saw Moses, the skin of his face was shining, and they were afraid to come near him.
31 But Moses called to them; and Aaron and all the leaders of the congregation returned to him, and Moses spoke with them.
32 Afterward all the Israelites came near, and he gave them in commandment all that the LORD had spoken with him on Mount Sinai.
33 When Moses had finished speaking with them, he put a veil on his face;
34 but whenever Moses went in before the LORD to speak with him, he would take the veil off, until he came out; and when he came out, and told the Israelites what he had been commanded,
35 the Israelites would see the face of Moses, that the skin of his face was shining; and Moses would put the veil on his face again, until he went in to speak with him.

Moses - Bringing Sexy Back

Musings

Moses returns from Sinai with the second copy of the ten commandments, after yet another 40-day period. He has been talking with God so much that his face glows. Instead of sunglasses, depicted here, he uses a vale when not speaking to the people or God. This is the only place a vale is mentioned in this context, so it either wasn't a reoccurring problem or it may have been preserved from another tradition.

Leviticus

Leviticus 19

The Golden Rule

The LORD spoke to Moses, saying: 2 Speak to all the congregation of the people of Israel and say to them: You shall be
holy, for I the LORD your God am holy. 3 You shall each revere your mother and father, and you shall keep my sab-
baths: I am the LORD your God. 4 Do not turn to idols or make cast images for yourselves: I am the LORD your God.
5 When you offer a sacrifice of well-being to the LORD, offer it in such a way that it is acceptable on your behalf. 6 It shall
be eaten on the same day you offer it, or on the next day; and anything left over until the third day shall be consumed in
fire. 7 If it is eaten at all on the third day, it is an abomination; it will not be acceptable. 8 All who eat it shall be subject to
punishment, because they have profaned what is holy to the LORD; and any such person shall be cut off from the peo-
ple. 9 When you reap the harvest of your land, you shall not reap to the very edges of your field, or gather the gleanings
of your harvest. 10 You shall not strip your vineyard bare, or gather the fallen grapes of your vineyard; you shall leave
them for the poor and the alien:
I am the LORD your God. 11 You
shall not steal; you shall not deal
falsely; and you shall not lie to
one another. 12 And you shall not
swear falsely by my name, pro-
faning the name of your God: I
am the LORD. 13 You shall not
defraud your neighbor; you shall
not steal; and you shall not keep
for yourself the wages of a labor-
er until morning. 14 You shall not
revile the deaf or put a stumbling
block before the blind; you shall
fear your God: I am the LORD.
15 You shall not render an unjust
judgment; you shall not be par-
tial to the poor or defer to the
great: with justice you shall judge
your neighbor. 16 You shall not go
around as a slanderer among
your people, and you shall not
profit by the blood of your neigh-
bor: I am the LORD. 17 You shall
not hate in your heart anyone of
your kin; you shall reprove your
neighbor, or you will incur guilt
yourself. 18 You shall not take
vengeance or bear a grudge against any of your people, but you shall love your neighbor as yourself: I am the LORD.
19 You shall keep my statutes. You shall not let your animals breed with a different kind; you shall not sow your field
with two kinds of seed; nor shall you put on a garment made of two different materials.

Headline: Golden Rule Holy - Not Full of Holes

Musings

Well, in case God hadn't made it perfectly clear, here are the Ten Commandments, plus a few, all over again. Verse 18 "love your neighbor as yourself" is probably the oldest version of the Golden Rule in the Bible and sort of a one-phrase summary of the last 5 of the 10 Commandments (the civil laws). Taking in all of Chapter 19, living a holy life means following God's commandments and trying to emulate God.

Numbers

Numbers 11

The Dad's Have It

[24] So Moses went out and told the people the words of the LORD; and he gathered seventy elders of the people, and placed them all around the tent. [25] Then the LORD came down in the cloud and spoke to him, and took some of the spirit that was on him and put it on the seventy elders; and when the spirit rested upon them, they prophesied. But they did not do so again. [26] Two men remained in the camp, one named Eldad, and the other named Medad, and the spirit rested on them; they were among those registered, but they had not gone out to the tent, and so they prophesied in the camp. [27] And a young man ran and told Moses, "Eldad and Medad are prophesying in the camp." [28] And Joshua son of Nun, the assistant of Moses, one of his chosen men, said, "My lord Moses, stop them!" [29] But Moses said to him, "Are you jealous for my sake? Would that all the Lord's people were prophets, and that the LORD would put his spirit on them!" [30] And Moses and the elders of Israel returned to the camp.

Oh Dad!

Musings

Moses selects 70 elders to share some of his responsibilities. There is a similar account in Exodus 18:13-26, but in that story Moses father-in-law suggests it and the 70 become judges. Here they meet and temporarily receive the gift of prophesy. Eldad and Medad didn't make the main meeting, no reason is given, but still received the gift of the spirit at the same time as the others. Joshua is worried that this somehow will compete with Moses' authority, but Moses is clearly not worried; in fact he would prefer it if more people would share in these responsibilities. A lesser leader might jealously guard his relationship with God and responsibility that came with it, but Moses would have preferred more help. He didn't want the role originally, and has no problem spreading the wealth.

Numbers 27
Josh Gets the Nod

12 The LORD said to Moses, "Go up this mountain of the Abarim range, and see the land that I have given to the Israelites. 13
When you have seen it, you also shall be gathered to your people, as your brother Aaron was, 14 because you rebelled against
my word in the wilderness of Zin when the congregation quarreled with me. You did not show my holiness before their eyes
at the waters." (These are the waters of Meribah-kadesh in the wilderness of Zin.) 15 Moses spoke to the LORD, saying, 16
"Let the LORD, the God of the spirits of all flesh, appoint someone over the congregation 17 who shall go out before them and
come in before them, who shall lead them out and bring them in, so that the congregation of the LORD may not be like sheep
without a shepherd." 18 So the LORD said to Moses, "Take Joshua son of Nun, a man in whom is the spirit, and lay your hand
upon him; 19 have him stand before Eleazar the priest and all the congregation, and commission him in their sight. 20 You
shall give him some of your authority, so that all the congregation of the Israelites may obey. 21 But he shall stand before Eleazar the priest, who shall inquire for him by the decision of the Urim before the LORD; at his word they shall go out, and at his word they shall come in, both he and all the Israelites with him, the whole congregation." 22 So Moses did as the LORD commanded him. He took Joshua and had him stand before Eleazar the priest and the whole congregation; 23 he laid his hands on him and commissioned him--as the LORD had directed through Moses.

Your Moment of "Zin"

Musings

Numbers 20:1-13 is a second and different account of Exodus 17:1-7 regarding the "tap" water of Meribah-kadesh, but a very important difference indeed. The prevailing thought is that God was angry with Aaron and Moses either for doubting that God would bring water out from the rock or the way in which they carried it out (in the Numbers he said "we" meaning Aaron and Moses, rather than God, would bring them water from the rock) or both. It seems like there should be more to it than that, yet this passage bears the consequences that Aaron and Moses would not get to cross over into the promised land with their people. Moses asks for a successor, God chooses Joshua, and has Moses give him "some" of his authority. The Urim (usually used in conjunction with the Thummim) was a sacred lot used in divination. This is very odd since Judaism is strongly against divination (most of the time). Here God already directed Moses on the matter, so perhaps it was just for show or added confirmation, but still unusual. In Exodus 28:30 the Urim and Thummim are put next to Aaron's heart, so perhaps this is more of a symbolic transfer of power or priesthood. One thing is clear, Joshua is a good choice, but it seems likely that he will not be as powerful or have as direct access to God as Moses.

Deuteronomy

Deuteronomy 4

How Great is Our God!

32 For ask now about former ages, long before your own, ever since the day that God created human beings on the earth;
ask from one end of heaven to the other: has anything so great as this ever happened or has its like ever been heard of?
33 Has any people ever heard the voice of a god speaking out of a fire, as you have heard, and lived? 34 Or has any god
ever attempted to go and take a nation for himself from the midst of another nation, by trials, by signs and wonders,
by war, by a mighty hand and an outstretched arm, and by terrifying displays of power, as the LORD your God did for
you in Egypt before your very eyes? 35 To you it was shown so that you would acknowledge that the LORD is God; there
is no other besides him. 36 From heaven he made you hear his voice to discipline you. On earth he showed you his great
fire, while you heard his words coming out of the fire. 37 And because he loved your ancestors, he chose their descen-
dants after them. He brought you out of Egypt with his own presence, by his great power,
38 driving out before you nations greater and mightier than yourselves, to bring you in, giving you their land for a possession, as it is still today.
39 So acknowledge today and take to heart that the LORD is God in heaven above and on the earth beneath; there is no other.
40 Keep his statutes and his commandments, which I am commanding you today for your own well-being and that of your descendants after you, so that you may long remain in the land that the LORD your God is giving you for all time.

Moses The Golden Years

Musings

Moses is a pretty good motivational speaker. In fact we find Moses doing most of the talking even though Aaron was appointed as his press secretary - perhaps that was for all the teaching and detail work and not the speeches. Moses reminds the Israelites just how miraculous the exodus is and that they were there for it. Very awesome, including some inside peeks at God that normally would result in instant death. God messed with Pharaoh, talked to them through fire, led them through the dessert, fed them, gave them the law and a land. Pretty amazing stuff.

Deuteronomy 6

The Proper Use of Merchandising

Now this is the commandment--the statutes and the ordinances--that the LORD your God charged me to teach you to

Teaching the Commandments

observe in the land that you are
about to cross into and occupy,
2 so that you and your children
and your children's children may
fear the LORD your God all the
days of your life, and keep all his
decrees and his commandments
that I am commanding you, so
that your days may be long. 3
Hear therefore, O Israel, and
observe them diligently, so that
it may go well with you, and so
that you may multiply greatly
in a land flowing with milk and
honey, as the LORD, the God
of your ancestors, has promised
you. 4 Hear, O Israel: The LORD
is our God, the LORD alone. 5
You shall love the LORD your
God with all your heart, and
with all your soul, and with all
your might. 6 Keep these words
that I am commanding you to-
day in your heart. 7 Recite them
to your children and talk about
them when you are at home and
when you are away, when you lie
down and when you rise. 8 Bind
them as a sign on your hand, fix them as an emblem on your forehead, 9 and write them on the door posts of your
house and on your gates.

Musings

This is a very important passage in Judaism, called the "Shema" (verses 4-9), and is a key exposition on the 1st commandment (and/or 2nd commandment depending on how you number them). It is also distinguished by verse 5, "You shall love the LORD your God with all your heart, and with all your soul, and with all your might" as a very important interpretation, centuries later referred to by Jesus as greatest of all the commandments. The idea of loving God so passionately as a positive motivator to keep the law stands in welcome contrast to doing so out of fear, obligation or even awe.

The cartoon has some fun with Moses as if he were merchandising scripture on doorposts, jewelry and headbands, but unlike the cartoon cool stuff sold at www.the-cartoonist.com web site, (What! Another shameless plug!) it was used as a teaching tool. It became a tradition and is still done to this day.

Note: the giving of the Ten Commandments is recorded in Deuteronomy Chapter 5, just before this passage, and also in Exodus Chapter 20. A good homework exercise would be to compare the two versions side-by-side. There may be a test.

Deuteronomy 18
No Magic Dudes

9 When you come into the land that the LORD your God is giving you, you must not learn to imitate the abhorrent practices of those nations. 10 No one shall be found among you who makes a son or daughter pass through fire, or who practices divination, or is a soothsayer, or an augur, or a sorcerer, 11 or one who casts spells, or who consults ghosts or spirits, or who seeks oracles from the dead. 12 For whoever does these things is abhorrent to the LORD; it is because of such abhorrent practices that the LORD your God is driving them out before you. 13 You must remain completely loyal to the LORD your God. 14 Although these nations that you are about to dispossess do give heed to soothsayers and diviners, as for you, the LORD your God does not permit you to do so. 15 The LORD your God will raise up for you a prophet like me from among your own people; you shall heed such a prophet. 16 This is what you requested of the LORD your God at Horeb on the day of the assembly when you said: "If I hear the voice of the LORD my God any more, or ever again see this great fire, I will die." 17 Then the LORD replied to me: "They are right in what they have said. 18 I will raise up for them a prophet like you from among their own people; I will put my words in the mouth of the prophet, who shall speak to them everything that I command. 19 Anyone who does not heed the words that the prophet shall speak in my name, I myself will hold accountable. 20 But any prophet who speaks in the name of other gods, or who presumes to speak in my name a word that I have not commanded the prophet to speak--that prophet shall die." 21 You may say to yourself, "How can we recognize a word that the LORD has not spoken?" 22 If a prophet speaks in the name of the LORD but the thing does not take place or prove true, it is a word that the LORD has not spoken. The prophet has spoken it presumptuously; do not be frightened by it.

No Clowing Around

Musings

This understanding of determining what is from God and what isn't is nothing less than enlightened for its time. First, it dispels any credibility in false idols, false gods, divination, magic, soothsaying, sorcery and child sacrifice. Cultures all around them practiced these things yet they understand it as just superstition. With that out of the way, this addresses how to tell if a prophet is a true profit of the LORD. A true prophet is like Moses, conveying ideas and principals consistent with the commandments. False prophets are those who intentionally (deceit) or unintentionally (self-delusion) preach false teachings or inaccurate predictions. The Israelites have the laws and instruction from God that are the measure of truth for them. They stand for something so they won't fall for just anything (in theory anyway). What a great advantage to have this as a nation.

Deuteronomy 26

First Fruits

When you have come into the land that the LORD your God is giving you as an inheritance to possess, and you pos-
sess it, and settle in it, 2 *you shall take some of the first of all the fruit of the ground, which you harvest from the land*
that the LORD your God is giving you, and you shall put it in a basket and go to the place that the LORD your God
will choose as a dwelling for his name. 3 *You shall go to the priest who is in office at that time, and say to him, "Today I*
declare to the LORD your God that I have come into the land that the LORD swore to our ancestors to give us." 4 *When*
the priest takes the basket from your hand and sets it down before the altar of the LORD your God, 5 *you shall make*
this response before the LORD your God: "A wandering Aramean was my ancestor; he went down into Egypt and lived
there as an alien, few in number, and there he became a great nation, mighty and populous. 6 *When the Egyptians*
treated us harshly and afflicted us, by imposing hard labor on us, 7 *we cried to the LORD, the God of our ancestors;*
the LORD heard our voice and saw our affliction, our toil, and our oppression. 8 *The LORD brought us out of Egypt*
with a mighty hand and an outstretched arm, with a terrifying display of power, and with signs and wonders; 9 *and*
he brought us into this place and gave us this land, a land flowing with milk and honey. 10 *So now I bring the first of*
the fruit of the ground that you, O LORD, have given me." You shall set it down before the LORD your God and bow
down before the LORD your God. 11 *Then you, together with the Levites and the aliens who reside among you, shall*
celebrate with all the bounty that the LORD your God has given to you and to your house.

Nut 'n' Honey

Musings

This is the offering of the first fruits of the harvest and was also a mini history lesson (at least from Jacob to their current time) in national identity. In a largely illiterate society these kinds of things help pass on the information from generation to generation.

Deuteronomy 30
Choose Life

11 Surely, this commandment that I am commanding you today is not too hard for you, nor is it too far away. 12 It is not in
heaven, that you should say, "Who will go up to heaven for us, and get it for us so that we may hear it and observe it?" 13
Neither is it beyond the sea, that you should say, "Who will cross to the other side of the sea for us, and get it for us so that
we may hear it and observe it?" 14 No, the word is very near to you; it is in your mouth and in your heart for you to observe.
15 See, I have set before you today life and prosperity, death and adversity. 16 If you obey the commandments of the LORD
your God that I am commanding you today, by loving the LORD your God, walking in his ways, and observing his com-
mandments, decrees, and ordinances, then you shall live and become numerous, and the LORD your God will bless you in
the land that you are entering to possess. 17 But if your heart turns away and you do not hear, but are led astray to bow down
to other gods and serve them, 18 I declare to you today that you shall perish; you shall not live long in the land that you are
crossing the Jordan to enter and possess. 19 I call heaven and earth to witness against you today that I have set before you
life and death, blessings and curses. Choose life so that you and your descendants may live, 20 loving the LORD your God,
obeying him, and holding fast to him; for that means life to you and length of days, so that you may live in the land that the
LORD swore to give to your ancestors, to Abraham, to Isaac, and to Jacob.

Great Comedy Teams of B.C.: Moses and Jack Benny

Musings

Normally a cartoon should not draw on period-related humor, but this passage is reflected so well in classic trademark humor of Jack Benny, a well-known comedian the second half of the twentieth century. Jack Benny had a comedic reputation of being such a tightwad that given a choice (by a mugger) of surrendering his wallet or his life, he had to think about it. That's the choice presented in this passage - live according to God's ways or else suffer the consequences. While it seems like an easy choice on paper, choosing incorrectly seems to happen repeatedly in the Bible so it is a fair warning.

Deuteronomy 34

I Told You We'd Get Here!

*Then Moses went up from the plains of Moab to Mount Nebo, to the top of Pisgah, which is opposite Jericho, and the
LORD showed him the whole land: Gilead as far as Dan, [2] all Naphtali, the land of Ephraim and Manasseh, all the
land of Judah as far as the Western Sea, [3] the Negeb, and the Plain--that is, the valley of Jericho, the city of palm trees-
-as far as Zoar. [4] The LORD said to him, "This is the land of which I swore to Abraham, to Isaac, and to Jacob, saying,
'I will give it to your descendants'; I have let you see it with your eyes, but you shall not cross over there." [5] Then Moses,
the servant of the LORD, died there in the land of Moab, at the Lord's command. [6] He was buried in a valley in the
land of Moab, opposite Beth-peor, but no one knows his burial place to this day. [7] Moses was one hundred twenty years
old when he died; his sight was unimpaired and his vigor had not abated. [8] The Israelites wept for Moses in the plains
of Moab thirty days; then the period of mourning for Moses was ended. [9] Joshua son of Nun was full of the spirit of
wisdom, because Moses had laid his hands on him; and the Israelites obeyed him, doing as the LORD had commanded
Moses. [10] Never since has there arisen a prophet in Israel like Moses, whom the LORD knew face to face. [11] He was un-
equaled for all the signs and wonders that the LORD sent him to perform in the land of Egypt, against Pharaoh and
all his servants and his entire land, [12] and for all the mighty deeds and all the terrifying displays of power that Moses
performed in the sight of all Israel.*

Tribute to a Prophet

Musings

This is essentially Moses obituary. Mostly Moses is remembered for his deeds and close relationship with God. Whether Moses saw the face of God or not is debatable (Num 12:28 versus Exodus 33:20), but clearly Moses had a pretty close audience with God. He was also pretty healthy to the last of his 127 years.

Joshua

Joshua 5:1-8

Cut to the Chase

When all the kings of the Amorites beyond the Jordan to the west, and all the kings of the Canaanites by the sea, heard that the
LORD had dried up the waters of the Jordan for the Israelites until they had crossed over, their hearts melted, and there was no
longer any spirit in them, because of the Israelites. 2 At that time the LORD said to Joshua, "Make flint knives and circumcise the
Israelites a second time." 3 So Joshua made flint knives, and circumcised the Israelites at Gibeath-haaraloth. 4 This is the reason
why Joshua circumcised them: all the males of the people who came out of Egypt, all the warriors, had died during the journey
through the wilderness after they had come out of Egypt. 5 Although all the people who came out had been circumcised, yet all the
people born on the journey through the wilderness after they had come out of Egypt had not been circumcised. 6 For the Israelites
traveled forty years in the wilderness, until all the nation, the warriors who came out of Egypt, perished, not having listened to

Being a Woman Has Its Advantages

the voice of the LORD. To them the LORD swore that he would not let them see the land that he had sworn to their ancestors to
give us, a land flowing with milk and honey. 7 So it was their children, whom he raised up in their place, that Joshua circumcised;
for they were uncircumcised, because they had not been circumcised on the way. 8 When the circumcising of all the nation was
done, they remained in their places in the camp until they were healed.

Musings

Well this is just one of those practices that is hard to fathom the reason of it other than hygiene. Circumcision was widely practiced in the region so it was not unique to the Israelites; however it is definitely observed as part of the covenant between God and Israel (initiated under Abraham), so it holds a place of prominence. There is speculation that the Egyptians may not have circumcised enough of the foreskin and thus a redo was in order; and it's unclear why it was not practiced during the exodus, but it wasn't. A fun fact "Gibeath-haaraloth" means "Foreskins Hill." Hard not to chuckle at that!

Joshua 5:9-12

Manna We Glad There's No More Manna!

*[9] The LORD said to Joshua, "Today I have rolled away from you the disgrace of Egypt." And so that place is called
Gilgal to this day. [10] While the Israelites were camped in Gilgal they kept the passover in the evening on the fourteenth
day of the month in the plains of Jericho. [11] On the day after the passover, on that very day, they ate the produce of the
land, unleavened cakes and parched grain. [12] The manna ceased on the day they ate the produce of the land, and the
Israelites no longer had manna; they ate the crops of the land of Canaan that year.*

Manna Crop Out

Musings

Timing is everything. They can start eating from the land, so they no longer need or have any manna. Probably none too soon for the folks who had been eating it for 40 years. Even a favorite food would be hard pressed to stay even tolerable that long, although still a blessing and better than starving. Gilgal not surprisingly means "to roll away."

Ruth

Ruth 1

Where Did All the Young Men Go? ... Long Time Passing

In the days when the judges ruled, there was a famine in the land, and a certain man of Bethlehem in Judah went to live in the country of
Moab, he and his wife and two sons. 2 The name of the man was Elimelech and the name of his wife Naomi, and the names of his two sons were
Mahlon and Chilion; they were Ephrathites from Bethlehem in Judah. They went into the country of Moab and remained there. 3 But Elimel-
ech, the husband of Naomi, died, and she was left with her two sons. 4 These took Moabite wives; the name of the one was Orpah and the name
of the other Ruth. When they had lived there about ten years, 5 both Mahlon and Chilion also died, so that the woman was left without her two
sons and her husband. 6 Then she started to return with her daughters-in-law from the country of Moab, for she had heard in the country of
Moab that the LORD had considered his people and given them food. 7 So she set out from the place where she had been living, she and her two
daughters-in-law, and they went on their way to go back to the land of Judah. 8 But Naomi said to her two daughters-in-law, "Go back each
of you to your mother's house. May the
LORD deal kindly with you, as you
have dealt with the dead and with me. 9
The LORD grant that you may find se-
curity, each of you in the house of your
husband." Then she kissed them, and
they wept aloud. 10 They said to her, "No,
we will return with you to your people."
11 But Naomi said, "Turn back, my
daughters, why will you go with me? Do
I still have sons in my womb that they
may become your husbands? 12 Turn
back, my daughters, go your way, for I
am too old to have a husband. Even if
I thought there was hope for me, even
if I should have a husband tonight and
bear sons, 13 would you then wait until
they were grown? Would you then re-
frain from marrying? No, my daughters,
it has been far more bitter for me than
for you, because the hand of the LORD
has turned against me." 14 Then they
wept aloud again. Orpah kissed her
mother-in-law, but Ruth clung to her.
15 So she said, "See, your sister-in-law
has gone back to her people and to her
gods; return after your sister-in-law."
16 But Ruth said, "Do not press me to
leave you or to turn back from follow-
ing you! Where you go, I will go; where
you lodge, I will lodge; your people shall
be my people, and your God my God. 17
Where you die, I will die-- there will I be
buried. May the LORD do thus and so
to me, and more as well, if even death parts me from you!" 18 When Naomi saw that she was determined to go with her, she said no more to
her. 19 So the two of them went on until they came to Bethlehem.

Through Thick and Thin

Musings

In the New Testament there is a parable call the "Prodigal Son" (Luke 15:11-32) which is really about the loving Father. In a similar sense the Book of Ruth is really the story of the redemption of Naomi. It has been suggested that this story also serves as a parable of how Naomi (aka how Israel acts - self-righteous and bitter) is redeemed through Ruth, the outsider (aka how Israel should act - loyal and loving). In this part of the story we see why Naomi is bitter, but Ruth is loyal and unrelenting. They are in this together.

Note: Notice the cartoon marginal character Adam has nothing to add to this story. Eve has exclusive coverage of the events.

Ruth 2

Barley Enough to Eat!

Now Naomi had a kinsman on her husband's side, a prominent rich man, of the family of Elimelech, whose name was
Boaz. 2 And Ruth the Moabite said to Naomi, "Let me go to the field and glean among the ears of grain, behind someone
in whose sight I may find favor." She said to her, "Go, my daughter." 3 So she went. She came and gleaned in the field be-
hind the reapers. As it happened, she came to the part of the field belonging to Boaz, who was of the family of Elimelech.
4 Just then Boaz came from Bethlehem. He said to the reapers, "The LORD be with you." They answered, "The LORD
bless you." 5 Then Boaz said to his servant who was in charge of the reapers, "To whom does this young woman belong?"
6 The servant who was in charge of the reapers answered, "She is the Moabite who came back with Naomi from the coun-
try of Moab. 7 She said, 'Please, let me glean and gather among the sheaves behind the reapers.' So she came, and she has

I Barley Know the Girl

been on her feet from early this
morning until now, without rest-
ing even for a moment." 8 Then
Boaz said to Ruth, "Now listen,
my daughter, do not go to glean
in another field or leave this one,
but keep close to my young wom-
en. 9 Keep your eyes on the field
that is being reaped, and follow
behind them. I have ordered the
young men not to bother you. If
you get thirsty, go to the vessels
and drink from what the young
men have drawn." 10 Then she fell
prostrate, with her face to the
ground, and said to him, "Why
have I found favor in your sight,
that you should take notice of
me, when I am a foreigner?" 11
But Boaz answered her, "All that
you have done for your mother-
in-law since the death of your
husband has been fully told me,
and how you left your father and
mother and your native land and
came to a people that you did not
know before. 12 May the LORD
reward you for your deeds, and
may you have a full reward from the LORD, the God of Israel, under whose wings you have come for refuge!"

Musings

This is no chance meeting. Naomi has Ruth glean in the fields of Boaz, behind the harvesters, something the poor were allowed to do. However, Boaz already knows the story of their hardships, and shows extra kindness to Ruth. Beyond this his motives are not known, but this could be the beginning of a deeper relationship.

Ruth 3

Ruth Persuades Boaz

Naomi her mother-in-law said to her, "My daughter, I need to seek some security for you, so that it may be well with you. [2] Now here is our kinsman Boaz, with whose young women you have been working. See, he is winnowing barley tonight at the threshing floor. [3] Now wash and anoint yourself, and put on your best clothes and go down to the threshing floor; but do not make yourself known to the man until he has finished eating and drinking. [4] When he lies down, observe the place where he lies; then, go and uncover his feet and lie down; and he will tell you what to do." [5] She said to her, "All that you tell me I will do." [6] So she went down to the threshing floor and did just as her mother-in-law had instructed her. [7] When Boaz had eaten and drunk, and he was in a contented mood, he went to lie down at the end of the heap of grain. Then she came stealthily and uncovered his feet, and lay down. [8] At midnight the man was startled, and turned over, and there, lying at his feet, was a woman! [9] He said, "Who are you?" And she answered, "I am Ruth, your servant; spread your cloak over your servant, for you are next-of-kin." [10] He said, "May you be blessed by the LORD, my daughter; this last instance of your loyalty is better than the first; you have not gone after young men, whether poor or rich. [11] And now, my daughter, do not be afraid, I will do for you all that you ask, for all the assembly of my people know that you are a worthy woman. [12] But now, though it is true that I am a near kinsman, there is another kinsman more closely related than I. [13] Remain this night, and in the morning, if he will act as next-of-kin for you, good; let him do it. If he is not willing to act as next-of-kin for you, then, as the LORD lives, I will act as next-of-kin for you. Lie down until the morning." [14] So she lay at his feet until morning, but got up before one person could recognize another; for he said, "It must not be known that the woman came to the threshing floor." [15] Then he said, "Bring the cloak you are wearing and hold it out." So she held it, and he measured out six measures of barley, and put it on her back; then he went into the city. [16] She came to her mother-in-law, who said, "How did things go with you, my daughter?" Then she told her all that the man had done for her, [17] saying, "He gave me these six measures of barley, for he said, 'Do not go back to your mother-in-law empty-handed.'" [18] She replied, "Wait, my daughter, until you learn how the matter turns out, for the man will not rest, but will settle the matter today."

I Heard it Through the Grape Vine

Musings

This part of the story didn't make into the lectionary, but it is too fun to leave out. It is full of sexual innuendos, which is playfully suggestive without actually saying anything scandalous happened. See if you can pick them all out (hint: feet, threshing floor, cloak, overnight). The whole next-of-kin thing can also mean redeemer, so basically Boaz leaves this encounter to ask permission from Naomi's dead husband's next-of-kin for permission to marry Ruth.

Ruth 4

Boaz Secures a Wife and Ruth a Nation

[7] Now this was the custom in former times in Israel concerning redeeming and exchanging: to confirm a transaction,
the one took off a sandal and gave it to the other; this was the manner of attesting in Israel. [8] So when the next-of-kin
said to Boaz, "Acquire it for yourself," he took off his sandal. [9] Then Boaz said to the elders and all the people, "Today
you are witnesses that I have acquired from the hand of Naomi all that belonged to Elimelech and all that belonged to
Chilion and Mahlon. [10] I have also acquired Ruth the Moabite, the wife of Mahlon, to be my wife, to maintain the dead
man's name on his inheritance, in order that the name of the dead may not be cut off from his kindred and from the
gate of his native place; today you are witnesses." [11] Then all the people who were at the gate, along with the elders, said,
"We are witnesses. May the LORD make the woman who is coming into your house like Rachel and Leah, who together
built up the house of Israel. May you produce children in Ephrathah and bestow a name in Bethlehem; [12] and, through

And They Lived Happily Ever After

the children that the LORD will
give you by this young woman,
may your house be like the house
of Perez, whom Tamar bore to
Judah." [13] So Boaz took Ruth and
she became his wife. When they
came together, the LORD made
her conceive, and she bore a son.
[14] Then the women said to Nao-
mi, "Blessed be the LORD, who
has not left you this day without
next-of-kin; and may his name
be renowned in Israel! [15] He shall
be to you a restorer of life and
a nourisher of your old age; for
your daughter-in-law who loves
you, who is more to you than sev-
en sons, has borne him." [16] Then
Naomi took the child and laid
him in her bosom, and became
his nurse. [17] The women of the
neighborhood gave him a name,
saying, "A son has been born to
Naomi." They named him Obed;
he became the father of Jesse, the
father of David. [18] Now these are
the descendants of Perez: Perez
became the father of Hezron, [19]
Hezron of Ram, Ram of Amminadab, [20] Amminadab of Nahshon, Nahshon of Salmon, [21] Salmon of Boaz, Boaz of
Obed, [22] Obed of Jesse, and Jesse of David.

Musings

Given that we accept the whole sandal exchange thing was a public acknowledgement that the "deal" was offered and accepted. Boaz is offering to take Ruth as a bride (for Naomi since she is past childbearing age) to carry on the line of Elimelech, Naomi's dead husband. The land Elimelech left behind when he went to Moab, currently used by the next-of-kin, would fall to Ruth's offspring. Basically Boaz' offer was "unless you want to take on the levirate marriage obligations to Naomi, I will." Apparently he didn't. Then the clincher: Ruth's offspring will lead all the way up to David, the greatest king of Israel. In the words of Paul Harvey: "and now you know the rest of the story."

Homework: find a good Bible commentary and look into the genealogy a bit more. It's interesting.

1st Samuel Excerpts

1st Samuel 2

Eli's Fertility Blessing

*18 Samuel was ministering before the LORD, a boy wearing a linen ephod. 19 His mother used to make for him a little
robe and take it to him each year, when she went up with her husband to offer the yearly sacrifice. 20 Then Eli would
bless Elkanah and his wife, and say, "May the LORD repay you with children by this woman for the gift that she made
to the LORD"; and then they would return to their home. 21 And the LORD took note of Hannah; she conceived and
bore three sons and two daughters. And the boy Samuel grew up in the presence of the LORD. 22 Now Eli was very old.
He heard all that his sons were doing to all Israel, and how they lay with the women who served at the entrance to the
tent of meeting. 23 He said to them, "Why do you do such things? For I hear of your evil dealings from all these people.
24 No, my sons; it is not a good report that I hear the people of the LORD spreading abroad. 25 If one person sins against
another, someone can intercede for the sinner with the LORD; but if someone sins against the LORD, who can make
intercession?" But they would not listen to the voice of their father; for it was the will of the LORD to kill them. 26 Now
the boy Samuel continued to grow both in stature and in favor with the LORD and with the people.*

Sam I Am

Musings

This is the origin story of Samuel. Verse 2:21 gives a quick recap of Chapter 1 where Hannah, who has been barren to that point, is praying for children. Sound familiar? She makes a vow that if God grants her children, her first will be dedicated to the LORD (raised in the temple) and essentially grow up as a servant to Eli. This has already happened by this passage, but is recounted and contrasted with Eli's own kids, who were derelicts. Samuel on the other hand grows "both in stature and in favor with the LORD and people." More than just a contrast to Eli's kids, Samuel is becoming a worthy successor to Eli. Not only is God smiling on him, but the people also like him.

1st Samuel 3

I Hear You Knocking

1 Now the boy Samuel was ministering to the LORD under Eli. The word of the LORD was rare in those days; visions were not widespread. 2 At that time Eli, whose eyesight had begun to grow dim so that he could not see, was lying down in his room; 3 the lamp of God had not yet gone out, and Samuel was lying down in the temple of the LORD, where the ark of God was. 4 Then the LORD called, "Samuel! Samuel!" and he said, "Here I am!" 5 and ran to Eli, and said, "Here I am, for you called me." But he said, "I did not call; lie down again." So he went and lay down. 6 The LORD called again, "Samuel!" Samuel got up and went to Eli, and said, "Here I am, for you called me." But he said, "I did not call, my son; lie down again." 7 Now Samuel did not yet know the LORD, and the word of the LORD had not yet been revealed to him. 8 The LORD called Samuel again, a third time. And he got up and went to Eli, and said, "Here I am, for you called me." Then Eli perceived that the LORD was calling the boy. 9 Therefore Eli said to Samuel, "Go, lie down; and if he calls you, you shall say, 'Speak, LORD, for your servant is listening.'" So Samuel went and lay down in his place. 10 Now the LORD came and stood there, calling as before, "Samuel! Samuel!" And Samuel said, "Speak, for your servant is listening." 11 Then the LORD said to Samuel, "See, I am about to do something in Israel that will make both ears of anyone who hears of it tingle. 12 On that day I will fulfill against Eli all that I have spoken concerning his house, from beginning to end. 13 For I have told him that I am about to punish his house forever, for the iniquity that he knew, because his sons were blaspheming God, and he did not restrain them. 14 Therefore I swear to the house of Eli that the iniquity of Eli's house shall not be expiated by sacrifice or offering forever." 15 Samuel lay there until morning; then he opened the doors of the house of the LORD. Samuel was afraid to tell the vision to Eli. 16 But Eli called Samuel and said, "Samuel, my son." He said, "Here I am." 17 Eli said, "What was it that he told you? Do not hide it from me. May God do so to you and more also, if you hide anything from me of all that he told you." 18 So Samuel told him everything and hid nothing from him. Then he said, "It is the LORD; let him do what seems good to him." 19 As Samuel grew up, the LORD was with him and let none of his words fall to the ground. 20 And all Israel from Dan to Beer-sheba knew that Samuel was a trustworthy prophet of the LORD. 21 The LORD continued to appear at Shiloh, for the LORD revealed himself to Samuel at Shiloh by the word of the LORD.

Knock, Knock. Who's There?

Musings

Just as the last passage was the origin of Samuel, this is his call. The response "Here I am" rings familiar to Abraham and Moses, and here it is spoken by Samuel to Eli. Calling three times simply emphasizes that it really is God calling, although in this situation it also has a very good comedic effect. Once the confusion about just who is calling is cleared up, Samuel responds to God and he is called to be a prophet and leader. Good for Samuel, bad for Eli. Eli wasn't surprised; it simply confirms what God had already told him would happen.

1st Samuel 8

Israel's Folly

[1] When Samuel became old, he made his sons judges over Israel. [2] The name of his firstborn son was Joel, and the name of his second, Abijah; they were judges in Beer-sheba. [3] Yet his sons did not follow in his ways, but turned aside after gain; they took bribes and perverted justice. [4] Then all the elders of Israel gathered together and came to Samuel at Ramah, [5] and said to him, "You are old and your sons do not follow in your ways; appoint for us, then, a king to govern us, like other nations." [6] But the thing displeased Samuel when they said, "Give us a king to govern us." Samuel prayed to the LORD, [7] and the LORD said to Samuel, "Listen to the voice of the people in all that they say to you; for they have not rejected you, but they have rejected me from being king over them. [8] Just as they have done to me, from the day I brought them up out of Egypt to this day, forsaking me and serving other gods, so also they are doing to you. [9] Now then, listen to their voice; only--you shall solemnly warn them, and show them the ways of the king who shall reign over them." [10] So Samuel reported all the words of the LORD to the people who were asking him for a king. [11] He said, "These will be the ways of the king who will reign over you: he will take your sons and appoint them to his chariots and to be his horsemen, and to run before his chariots; [12] and he will appoint for himself commanders of thousands and commanders of fifties, and some to plow his ground and to reap his harvest, and to make his implements of war and the equipment of his chariots. [13] He will take your daughters to be perfumers and cooks and bakers. [14] He will take the best of your fields and vineyards and olive orchards and give them to his courtiers. [15] He will take one-tenth of your grain and of your vineyards and give it to his officers and his courtiers. [16] He will take your male and female slaves, and the best of your cattle and donkeys, and put them to his work. [17] He will take one-tenth of your flocks, and you shall be his slaves. [18] And in that day you will cry out because of your king, whom you have chosen for yourselves; but the LORD will not answer you in that day." [19] But the people refused to listen to the voice of Samuel; they said, "No! but we are determined to have a king over us, [20] so that we also may be like other nations, and that our king may govern us and go out before us and fight our battles." [21] When Samuel had heard all the words of the people, he repeated them in the ears of the LORD. [22] The LORD said to Samuel, "Listen to their voice and set a king over them." Samuel then said to the people of Israel, "Each of you return home."

What Could Go Wrong?

Musings

What is it with kids anyway? Eli's kids were evil and now Samuel's kids were corrupt as well. The people turn to Samuel for a king. A judge had many roles - prophet, military leader, judge (law giver and decider) and as such was sort of a mini-king already. So the people may be thinking a king is a natural extension of a judge; Samuel warns them to the contrary. God seems almost ambivalent suggesting that the people will do what they want whether it's God's will or not. This doesn't seem like the God who was leading them through the dessert, but ultimately tells Samuel to give them what they want. The irony is that all the negative things Samuel tells them about a king come true. Under the category of "be careful what you ask for" - they desired to "be like other nations" and they will get their wish.

1st Samuel 16

Cinderella

1 The LORD said to Samuel, "How long will you grieve over Saul? I have rejected him from being king over Israel. Fill
your horn with oil and set out; I will send you to Jesse the Bethlehemite, for I have provided for myself a king among
his sons." 2 Samuel said, "How can I go? If Saul hears of it, he will kill me." And the LORD said, "Take a heifer with you,
and say, 'I have come to sacrifice to the LORD.' 3 Invite Jesse to the sacrifice, and I will show you what you shall do; and
you shall anoint for me the one whom I name to you." 4 Samuel did what the LORD commanded, and came to Beth-
lehem. The elders of the city came to meet him trembling, and said, "Do you come peaceably?" 5 He said, "Peaceably; I
have come to sacrifice to the LORD; sanctify yourselves and come with me to the sacrifice." And he sanctified Jesse and
his sons and invited them to the sacrifice. 6 When they came, he looked on Eliab and thought, "Surely the Lord's anoint-
ed is now before the LORD." 7
But the LORD said to Samuel,
"Do not look on his appearance
or on the height of his stature,
because I have rejected him; for
the LORD does not see as mor-
tals see; they look on the outward
appearance, but the LORD looks
on the heart." 8 Then Jesse called
Abinadab, and made him pass
before Samuel. He said, "Neither
has the LORD chosen this one."
9 Then Jesse made Shammah
pass by. And he said, "Neither
has the LORD chosen this one."
10 Jesse made seven of his sons
pass before Samuel, and Samuel
said to Jesse, "The LORD has not
chosen any of these." 11 Samuel
said to Jesse, "Are all your sons
here?" And he said, "There re-
mains yet the youngest, but he is
keeping the sheep." And Samuel
said to Jesse, "Send and bring
him; for we will not sit down
until he comes here." 12 He sent
and brought him in. Now he was
ruddy, and had beautiful eyes,
and was handsome. The LORD
said, "Rise and anoint him; for
this is the one." 13 Then Samuel took the horn of oil, and anointed him in the presence of his brothers; and the spirit of
the LORD came mightily upon David from that day forward. Samuel then set out and went to Ramah.

How to Disappoint a Fatted Calf

Musings

God is apparently good at covert operations, instructing Samuel on how to find the new king without arousing suspicion in Saul. By the way, the lectionary pretty much skips over the Saul story, focusing more on David, hence the big jump to Chapter 16. The good news is God judges a person by their heart, not their outward appearance, and selects the youngest of Jesse's sons - David. Turns out David also had all the outward appearance working for him, but it wasn't part of the criteria. Samuel (and God) seem to follow the same process in selecting David that they used to select Saul. Samuel probably wonders if David will work out any better. After all, he warned the people about kings.

1st Samuel 16

Star Search

14 Now the spirit of the LORD departed from Saul, and an evil spirit from the LORD tormented him. 15 And Saul's
servants said to him, "See now, an evil spirit from God is tormenting you. 16 Let our lord now command the servants
who attend you to look for someone who is skillful in playing the lyre; and when the evil spirit from God is upon you,
he will play it, and you will feel better." 17 So Saul said to his servants, "Provide for me someone who can play well, and
bring him to me." 18 One of the young men answered, "I have seen a son of Jesse the Bethlehemite who is skillful in play-
ing, a man of valor, a warrior, prudent in speech, and a man of good presence; and the LORD is with him." 19 So Saul
sent messengers to Jesse, and said, "Send me your son David who is with the sheep." 20 Jesse took a donkey loaded with
bread, a skin of wine, and a kid, and sent them by his son David to Saul. 21 And David came to Saul, and entered his
service. Saul loved him greatly, and he became his armor-bearer. 22 Saul sent to Jesse, saying, "Let David remain in my
service, for he has found favor in my sight." 23 And whenever the evil spirit from God came upon Saul, David took the
lyre and played it with his hand, and Saul would be relieved and feel better, and the evil spirit would depart from him.

Israeli Idol

Saul's expert panel of judges approve of David's soothing melodies ...

Musings

Well, Saul is out and Dave is in. Notice that the evil spirit tormenting Saul is from God. In the earlier books of the Old Testament everything comes from God including evil spirits (see also Pharaoh in Exodus). Some attribute the way Saul is acting to mental illness of some kind, which may well have been considered evil spirits back then. David is tasked with playing for Saul to soothe his troubles and also to be his armor-bearer. Saul becomes very fond of David although we don't know what David thinks of Saul. One wonders if this is like an apprenticeship for David, to be close enough to observe what kings do.

2nd Samuel

2nd Samuel 1

Thank You, Thank You Very Much

[1] After the death of Saul, when David had returned from defeating the Amalekites, David remained two days in Ziklag. [...]
[17] David intoned this lamentation over Saul and his son Jonathan. [18] (He ordered that The Song of the Bow be taught to the
people of Judah; it is written in the Book of Jashar.) He said: [19] Your glory, O Israel, lies slain upon your high places! How
the mighty have fallen! [20] Tell it not in Gath, proclaim it not in the streets of Ashkelon; or the daughters of the Philistines will
rejoice, the daughters of the uncircumcised will exult. [21] You mountains of Gilboa, let there be no dew or rain upon you, nor
bounteous fields! For there the shield of the mighty was defiled, the shield of Saul, anointed with oil no more. [22] From the
blood of the slain, from the fat of the mighty, the bow of Jonathan did not turn back, nor the sword of Saul return empty. [23]
Saul and Jonathan, beloved and lovely! In life and in death they were not divided; they were swifter than eagles, they were
stronger than lions. [24] O daughters of Israel, weep over Saul, who clothed you with crimson, in luxury, who put ornaments
of gold on your apparel. [25] How the mighty have fallen in the midst of the battle! Jonathan lies slain upon your high places.
[26] I am distressed for you, my brother Jonathan; greatly beloved were you to me; your love to me was wonderful, passing the
love of women. [27] How the mighty have fallen, and the weapons of war perished!

Karaoke's Early Roots

Musings

We skip over the huge drama that plays out between David and Saul and move to Saul's death and David's tribute to Saul and son, and David's dear friend, Jonathan. The bow was Jonathan's weapon of choice (the sword was Saul's) so even though it is a tribute to king Saul, it may be more in honor of Jonathan. The Philistines, who Saul was battling at the time of his death, remain a strong military threat to the region.

2nd Samuel 5:1-5

David's Inauguration Speech

1 Then all the tribes of Israel came to David at Hebron, and said, "Look, we are your bone and flesh. 2 For some time, while Saul was king over us, it was you who led out Israel and brought it in. The LORD said to you: It is you who shall be shepherd of my people Israel, you who shall be ruler over Israel." 3 So all the elders of Israel came to the king at Hebron; and King David made a covenant with them at Hebron before the LORD, and they anointed David king over Israel. 4 David was thirty years old when he began to reign, and he reigned forty years. 5 At Hebron he reigned over Judah seven years and six months; and at Jerusalem he reigned over all Israel and Judah thirty-three years.

David Humbly Accepts Supreme Dictatorship

Musings

It's hard to be humble when you are as great as David? Seven years after the death of Saul, David unites the kingdom under him. Samuel is long past at this point, but his warnings about kings should still resonate with Israel.

2nd Samuel 5:6-12

Dave Relocates

*6 The king and his men marched to Jerusalem against the Jebusites, the inhabitants of the land, who said to David,
"You will not come in here, even the blind and the lame will turn you back"--thinking, "David cannot come in here." 7
Nevertheless David took the stronghold of Zion, which is now the city of David. 8 David had said on that day, "Who-
ever would strike down the Jebusites, let him get up the water shaft to attack the lame and the blind, those whom Da-
vid hates." Therefore it is said, "The blind and the lame shall not come into the house." 9 David occupied the stronghold,
and named it the city of David. David built the city all around from the Millo inward. 10 And David became greater
and greater, for the LORD, the God of hosts, was with him. 11 King Hiram of Tyre sent messengers to David, along with
cedar trees, and carpenters and masons who built David a house. 12 David then perceived that the LORD had estab-
lished him king over Israel, and that he had exalted his kingdom for the sake of his people Israel.*

The House that David Built

Musings

This is very cryptic until it is revealed that this is a bit of school-yard taunts. The Jebusites are telling David that even their blind and lame will repel his soldiers if he attacks. David then takes the city with a small force that sneaks in through the water shaft. He who laughs last, laughs best. Jerusalem is a city central to the region and has the added benefit that it had not ever belonged to any of the 12 tribes, so he gets to claim it (aka the City of David). Donald Trump, eat your heart out.

2nd Samuel 6

David's Dance Party

1 David again gathered all the chosen men of Israel, thirty thousand. 2 David and all the people with him set out and
went from Baale-judah, to bring up from there the ark of God, which is called by the name of the LORD of hosts who is
enthroned on the cherubim. 3 They carried the ark of God on a new cart, and brought it out of the house of Abinadab,
which was on the hill. Uzzah and Ahio, the sons of Abinadab, were driving the new cart 4 with the ark of God; and Ahio
went in front of the ark. 5 David and all the house of Israel were dancing before the LORD with all their might, with
songs and lyres and harps and tambourines and castanets and cymbals. 6 When they came to the threshing floor of Na-
con, Uzzah reached out his hand to the ark of God and took hold of it, for the oxen shook it. 7 The anger of the LORD was
kindled against Uzzah; and God struck him there because he reached out his hand to the ark; and he died there beside
the ark of God. 8 David was angry because the LORD had burst forth with an outburst upon Uzzah; so that place is
called Perez-uzzah, to this day.
9 David was afraid of the LORD
that day; he said, "How can the
ark of the LORD come into my
care?" 10 So David was unwill-
ing to take the ark of the LORD
into his care in the city of Da-
vid; instead David took it to
the house of Obed-edom the
Gittite. 11 The ark of the LORD
remained in the house of Obed-
edom the Gittite three months;
and the LORD blessed Obed-
edom and all his household. 12
It was told King David, "The
LORD has blessed the house-
hold of Obed-edom and all that
belongs to him, because of the
ark of God." So David went and
brought up the ark of God from
the house of Obed-edom to the
city of David with rejoicing; 13
and when those who bore the
ark of the LORD had gone six
paces, he sacrificed an ox and a
fatling. 14 David danced before
the LORD with all his might;
David was girded with a linen
ephod. 15 So David and all the
house of Israel brought up the ark of the LORD with shouting, and with the sound of the trumpet.

Touchy!

Musings

This event is about midway through David's reign as king (20ish years). Talk about being in the wrong place at the wrong time - it appears that Uzzah's big mistake was that he wasn't ritually prepared to handle the sacred vessel ... so he got zapped. David apparently learns from this and makes sure they follow the proper procedures before bringing it on into the city. Bringing the ark into Jerusalem is a significant symbolic gesture, further identifying the city as the center of the nation.

2nd Samuel 7:1-17

God Prefers Camping

Now when the king was settled in his house, and the LORD had given him rest from all his enemies around him, 2 the
king said to the prophet Nathan, "See now, I am living in a house of cedar, but the ark of God stays in a tent." 3 Nathan
said to the king, "Go, do all that you have in mind; for the LORD is with you." 4 But that same night the word of the
LORD came to Nathan: 5 Go and tell my servant David: Thus says the LORD: Are you the one to build me a house to
live in? 6 I have not lived in a house since the day I brought up the people of Israel from Egypt to this day, but I have
been moving about in a tent and a tabernacle. 7 Wherever I have moved about among all the people of Israel, did I ever
speak a word with any of the tribal leaders of Israel, whom I commanded to shepherd my people Israel, saying, "Why
have you not built me a house of cedar?" 8 Now therefore thus you shall say to my servant David: Thus says the LORD
of hosts: I took you from the pasture, from following the sheep to be prince over my people Israel; 9 and I have been with
you wherever you went, and have cut off all your enemies from before you; and I will make for you a great name, like
the name of the great ones of the earth. 10 And I will appoint a place for my people Israel and will plant them, so that they
may live in their own place, and be disturbed no more; and evildoers shall afflict them no more, as formerly, 11 from the
time that I appointed judges over my people Israel; and I will give you rest from all your enemies. Moreover the LORD declares to you that the LORD will make you a house. 12 When
your days are fulfilled and you lie down with your ancestors, I will raise up your offspring after you, who shall come forth from your body, and I will establish his kingdom. 13 He shall
build a house for my name, and I will establish the throne of his kingdom forever. 14 I will
be a father to him, and he shall be a son to me. When he commits iniquity, I will punish him with a rod such as mortals use, with blows inflicted by human beings. 15 But I will not take my
steadfast love from him, as I took it from Saul, whom I put away from before you. 16 Your
house and your kingdom shall be made sure forever before me; your throne shall be established forever. 17 In accordance with all these words and with
all this vision, Nathan spoke to David.

You Rang?

Musings

David gets the idea that if he has a nice house, God would surely want one too. However, God seems to prefer camping for the moment. Later he will have Solomon build God a formal temple. Perhaps God did not like David's interior decorator or something. Enter Nathan, a prophet along the lines of Samuel and initially in favor of the temple, to be the messenger for God to tell David to wait.

2nd Samuel 7:18-29

David's House Prayer

18 Then King David went in and sat before the LORD, and said, "Who am I, O Lord GOD, and what is my house, that
you have brought me thus far? 19 And yet this was a small thing in your eyes, O Lord GOD; you have spoken also of
your servant's house for a great while to come. May this be instruction for the people, O Lord GOD! 20 And what more
can David say to you? For you know your servant, O Lord GOD! 21 Because of your promise, and according to your own
heart, you have wrought all this greatness, so that your servant may know it. 22 Therefore you are great, O LORD God;
for there is no one like you, and there is no God besides you, according to all that we have heard with our ears. 23 Who
is like your people, like Israel? Is there another nation on earth whose God went to redeem it as a people, and to make
a name for himself, doing great
and awesome things for them,
by driving out before his people
nations and their gods? 24 And
you established your people Is-
rael for yourself to be your peo-
ple forever; and you, O LORD,
became their God. 25 And now,
O LORD God, as for the word
that you have spoken concern-
ing your servant and concern-
ing his house, confirm it forev-
er; do as you have promised. 26
Thus your name will be magni-
fied forever in the saying, 'The
LORD of hosts is God over Is-
rael'; and the house of your ser-
vant David will be established
before you. 27 For you, O LORD
of hosts, the God of Israel, have
made this revelation to your
servant, saying, 'I will build you
a house'; therefore your servant
has found courage to pray this
prayer to you. 28 And now, O
Lord GOD, you are God, and
your words are true, and you
have promised this good thing
to your servant; 29 now therefore
may it please you to bless the house of your servant, so that it may continue forever before you; for you, O Lord GOD,
have spoken, and with your blessing shall the house of your servant be blessed forever."

There Is No One Like You

Musings

If for no other reason, David may be the greatest king of Israel because in his better moments he attributes everything to God, not only for his good fortune but for Israel's. This passage pays homage to YHWH (the LORD) as well as any passage in the Bible.

2nd Samuel 11

There Must Be 50 Ways to Leave Your Lover

1 In the spring of the year, the time when kings go out to battle, David sent Joab with his officers and all Israel with him; they
ravaged the Ammonites, and besieged Rabbah. But David remained at Jerusalem. 2 It happened, late one afternoon, when David
rose from his couch and was walking about on the roof of the king's house, that he saw from the roof a woman bathing; the woman
was very beautiful. 3 David sent someone to inquire about the woman. It was reported, "This is Bathsheba daughter of Eliam, the
wife of Uriah the Hittite." 4 So David sent messengers to get her, and she came to him, and he lay with her. (Now she was purifying
herself after her period.) Then she returned to her house. 5 The woman conceived; and she sent and told David, "I am pregnant." 6
So David sent word to Joab, "Send me Uriah the Hittite." And Joab sent Uriah to David. 7 When Uriah came to him, David asked
how Joab and the people fared, and how the war was going. 8 Then David said to Uriah, "Go down to your house, and wash your
feet." Uriah went out of the king's
house, and there followed him a
present from the king. 9 But Uriah
slept at the entrance of the king's
house with all the servants of his
lord, and did not go down to his
house. 10 When they told David,
"Uriah did not go down to his
house," David said to Uriah, "You
have just come from a journey.
Why did you not go down to your
house?" 11 Uriah said to David,
"The ark and Israel and Judah re-
main in booths; and my lord Joab
and the servants of my lord are
camping in the open field; shall I
then go to my house, to eat and to
drink, and to lie with my wife? As
you live, and as your soul lives, I
will not do such a thing." 12 Then
David said to Uriah, "Remain
here today also, and tomorrow
I will send you back." So Uriah
remained in Jerusalem that day.
On the next day, 13 David invited
him to eat and drink in his pres-
ence and made him drunk; and in
the evening he went out to lie on
his couch with the servants of his
lord, but he did not go down to
his house. 14 In the morning David
wrote a letter to Joab, and sent it by the hand of Uriah. 15 In the letter he wrote, "Set Uriah in the forefront of the hardest fighting,
and then draw back from him, so that he may be struck down and die."

Uriah In a Heap (of Trouble)

Musings

Probably one of the most damning passages in the Bible is here where king David commits adultery, tries to cover it up and finally has Uriah murdered. Uriah is blameless, he follows all of the proper loyalties and rituals of warfare, only in this case it works against him. It is clearly David's child as the comment about Bathsheba's purifying ritual reveals (otherwise too much information - TMI)! As good a king as David is as a military leader is just about as bad a king as he is when it comes to his personal life. This kind of information makes it very hard to like him. It's a tribute to the Bible not to show their leaders as flawless, perhaps suggesting that while God is perfect, people are not. It also goes a long way toward explaining why history didn't always work out as planned. David goes on to marry Bathsheba and the cover-up seems to be working, although there are lot of people privy to it (e.g., servants, Joab).

2nd Samuel 12:1-14

The Moral of the Story

1 and the LORD sent Nathan to David. He came to him, and said to him, "There were two men in a certain city, the one
rich and the other poor. 2 The rich man had very many flocks and herds; 3 but the poor man had nothing but one little
ewe lamb, which he had bought. He brought it up, and it grew up with him and with his children; it used to eat of his
meager fare, and drink from his cup, and lie in his bosom, and it was like a daughter to him. 4 Now there came a trav-
eler to the rich man, and he was loath to take one of his own flock or herd to prepare for the wayfarer who had come to
him, but he took the poor man's lamb, and prepared that for the guest who had come to him." 5 Then David's anger was
greatly kindled against the man. He said to Nathan, "As the LORD lives, the man who has done this deserves to die; 6 he
shall restore the lamb fourfold,
because he did this thing, and
because he had no pity." 7 Na-
than said to David, "You are
the man! Thus says the LORD,
the God of Israel: I anointed you
king over Israel, and I rescued
you from the hand of Saul; 8 I
gave you your master's house,
and your master's wives into
your bosom, and gave you the
house of Israel and of Judah;
and if that had been too little,
I would have added as much
more. 9 Why have you despised
the word of the LORD, to do
what is evil in his sight? You
have struck down Uriah the
Hittite with the sword, and
have taken his wife to be your
wife, and have killed him with
the sword of the Ammonites. 10
Now therefore the sword shall
never depart from your house,
for you have despised me, and
have taken the wife of Uriah the
Hittite to be your wife. 11 Thus
says the LORD: I will raise up
trouble against you from within
your own house; and I will take your wives before your eyes, and give them to your neighbor, and he shall lie with your
wives in the sight of this very sun. 12 For you did it secretly; but I will do this thing before all Israel, and before the sun."
13 David said to Nathan, "I have sinned against the LORD." Nathan said to David, "Now the LORD has put away your
sin; you shall not die. 14 Nevertheless, because by this deed you have utterly scorned the LORD, the child that is born
to you shall die."

A Grimm Fairy Tale

Musings

Not too much interpretation needed on this little story. David is caught, he repents, but the sentence he set for himself (or Nathan's rich man anyway) will be visited upon his and Bathsheba's child. So much for the perfect crime. We also have the prediction that as this went, so goes the rest of his family life. In other words, this is going to get ugly. David could have reacted in many ways to Nathan, including killing him, but he chooses to have Nathan become one of his most trusted advisors. Perhaps David understands that Nathan was also chosen by God.

2nd Samuel 12:15-24

Sincerely Disturbing

15 Then Nathan went to his house. The LORD struck the child that Uriah's wife bore to David, and it became very ill. 16
David therefore pleaded with God for the child; David fasted, and went in and lay all night on the ground. 17 The elders
of his house stood beside him, urging him to rise from the ground; but he would not, nor did he eat food with them. 18
On the seventh day the child died. And the servants of David were afraid to tell him that the child was dead; for they
said, "While the child was still alive, we spoke to him, and he did not listen to us; how then can we tell him the child is
dead? He may do himself some harm." 19 But when David saw that his servants were whispering together, he perceived
that the child was dead; and
David said to his servants, "Is
the child dead?" They said,
"He is dead." 20 Then David
rose from the ground, washed,
anointed himself, and changed
his clothes. He went into the
house of the LORD, and wor-
shiped; he then went to his own
house; and when he asked, they
set food before him and he ate.
21 Then his servants said to him,
"What is this thing that you
have done? You fasted and wept
for the child while it was alive;
but when the child died, you
rose and ate food." 22 He said,
"While the child was still alive, I
fasted and wept; for I said, 'Who
knows? The LORD may be gra-
cious to me, and the child may
live.' 23 But now he is dead; why
should I fast? Can I bring him
back again? I shall go to him,
but he will not return to me."
24 Then David consoled his wife
Bathsheba, and went to her, and
lay with her; and she bore a son,
and he named him Solomon.
The LORD loved him, ...

There's Got to be an After Mourning

Musings

David was pragmatic. He fasted and prayed for the child while alive, but once the baby died David returned to business as usual. Perhaps somewhat insensitive not to morn the child's death, yet he did all he could to save him and later actually consoles Bathsheba.

Time in the Bible is always interesting, it can go very slowly or it can jump months and years as serves the purposes of the story. David and Bathsheba have another child, Solomon, who will later take over as king, but is not mentioned again until much later. This jump in time is simply a way of wrapping up the story.

2nd Samuel 18:1-15

Accidents Will Happen

1 Then David mustered the men who were with him, and set over them commanders of thousands and commanders of hundreds.
5 The king ordered Joab and Abishai and Ittai, saying, "Deal gently for my sake with the young man Absalom." And all the people
heard when the king gave orders to all the commanders concerning Absalom. 9 Absalom happened to meet the servants of David.
Absalom was riding on his mule, and the mule went under the thick branches of a great oak. His head caught fast in the oak,
and he was left hanging between heaven and earth, while the mule that was under him went on. 10 A man saw it, and told Joab,
"I saw Absalom hanging in an oak." 11 Joab said to the man who told him, "What, you saw him! Why then did you not strike
him there to the ground? I would have been glad to give you ten pieces of silver and a belt." 12 But the man said to Joab, "Even if I
felt in my hand the weight of a thousand pieces of silver, I would not raise my hand against the king's son; for in our hearing the
king commanded you and Abishai and Ittai, saying: For my sake protect the young man Absalom! 13 On the other hand, if I had
dealt treacherously against his life (and there is nothing hidden from the king), then you yourself would have stood aloof." 14 Joab
said, "I will not waste time like this with you." He took three spears in his hand, and thrust them into the heart of Absalom, while
he was still alive in the oak. 15 And ten young men, Joab's armor-bearers, surrounded Absalom and struck him, and killed him.

Good to the Last Drop

Musings

David's family could have been fodder for raunchy daytime television shows - full of incest, rape, revenge and other low-life drama. Had David simply been able to apply the same standards to his family as he did to his country, there might have been a chance to avoid a lot of strife. Suffice it to say that Absalom, one of David's sons, is out of control and working to usurp David's throne and Joab, loyal military leader, isn't going to let that happen. Unfortunately for Absalom in his attempt to flee a battle he got stuck in a tree and became essentially a sitting duck. Joab and his men kill him.

2nd Samuel 18:24-33

Snail Mail

24 Now David was sitting between the two gates. The sentinel went up to the roof of the gate by the wall, and when he looked up, he
saw a man running alone. 25 The sentinel shouted and told the king. The king said, "If he is alone, there are tidings in his mouth."
He kept coming, and drew near. 26 Then the sentinel saw another man running; and the sentinel called to the gatekeeper and said,
"See, another man running alone!" The king said, "He also is bringing tidings." 27 The sentinel said, "I think the running of the
first one is like the running of Ahimaaz son of Zadok." The king said, "He is a good man, and comes with good tidings." 28 Then
Ahimaaz cried out to the king, "All is well!" He prostrated himself before the king with his face to the ground, and said, "Blessed
be the LORD your God, who has delivered up the men who raised their hand against my lord the king." 29 The king said, "Is it
well with the young man Absalom?" Ahimaaz answered, "When Joab sent your servant, I saw a great tumult, but I do not know
what it was." 30 The king said, "Turn aside, and stand here." So he turned aside, and stood still. 31 Then the Cushite came; and the
Cushite said, "Good tidings for my lord the king! For the LORD has vindicated you this day, delivering you from the power of all
who rose up against you." 32 The king said to the Cushite, "Is it well with the young man Absalom?" The Cushite answered, "May
the enemies of my lord the king, and all who rise up to do you harm, be like that young man." 33 The king was deeply moved, and
went up to the chamber over the gate, and wept; and as he went, he said, "O my son Absalom, my son, my son Absalom! Would
I had died instead of you, O Absalom, my son, my son!"

Delivering the Bad News

Musings

The only ones that cared about Absalom's death were David and the Northern tribes that were in on the attempted revolt. David mourns the death of Absalom, but Absalom had murdered Amnon, for raping their sister Tamar, and tried to displace David. Perhaps with good reason. However, with Absalom out of the picture, David goes on to rule the entire kingdom, North and South, so Joab's actions reunify the nation even if at David's emotional expense.

2nd Samuel 23

R.I.P. David

1 Now these are the last words of David: The oracle of David, son of Jesse, the oracle of the man whom God exalted, the anointed of the God of Jacob, the favorite of the Strong One of Israel: 2 The spirit of the LORD speaks through me, his word is upon my tongue. 3 The God of Israel has spoken, the Rock of Israel has said to me: One who rules over people justly, ruling in the fear of God, 4 is like the light of morning, like the sun rising on a cloudless morning, gleaming from the rain on the grassy land. 5 Is not my house like this with God? For he has made with me an everlasting covenant, ordered in all things and secure. Will he not cause to prosper all my help and my desire? 6 But the godless are all like thorns that are thrown away; for they cannot be picked up with the hand; 7 to touch them one uses an iron bar or the shaft of a spear. And they are entirely consumed in fire on the spot.

Parting Thoughts

Musings

David's parting thoughts are a fitting tribute to his tenure as king and God's blessing on him and Israel. While David is a terrible husband and parent, overall he's guided Israel to a unified kingdom and his heart always seemed to rest with God.

1st Kings

1st Kings 2

Next

*When David's time to die drew near, he charged his son Solomon, saying: [2] "I am about to go the way of all the earth.
Be strong, be courageous, [3] and keep the charge of the LORD your God, walking in his ways and keeping his statutes,
his commandments, his ordinances, and his testimonies, as it is written in the law of Moses, so that you may prosper in
all that you do and wherever you turn. [4] Then the LORD will establish his word that he spoke concerning me: 'If your
heirs take heed to their way, to walk before me in faithfulness with all their heart and with all their soul, there shall not
fail you a successor on the throne of Israel.' [5] "Moreover you know also what Joab son of Zeruiah did to me, how he dealt
with the two commanders of the armies of Israel, Abner son of Ner, and Amasa son of Jether, whom he murdered, re-
taliating in time of peace for blood that had been shed in war, and putting the blood of war on the belt around his waist,*

David's Second to the Last Words

*and on the sandals on his feet. [6]
Act therefore according to your
wisdom, but do not let his gray
head go down to Sheol in peace.
[7] Deal loyally, however, with the
sons of Barzillai the Gileadite,
and let them be among those
who eat at your table; for with
such loyalty they met me when I
fled from your brother Absalom.
[8] There is also with you Shimei
son of Gera, the Benjaminite
from Bahurim, who cursed me
with a terrible curse on the day
when I went to Mahanaim; but
when he came down to meet me
at the Jordan, I swore to him by
the LORD, 'I will not put you to
death with the sword.' [9] There-
fore do not hold him guiltless,
for you are a wise man; you will
know what you ought to do to
him, and you must bring his
gray head down with blood to
Sheol." [10] Then David slept with
his ancestors, and was buried
in the city of David. [11] The time
that David reigned over Israel
was forty years; he reigned sev-
en years in Hebron, and thirty-three years in Jerusalem. [12] So Solomon sat on the throne of his father David; and his
kingdom was firmly established.*

Musings

Again we have David on his deathbed, this time providing instructions to Solomon on how to lead, including a set of instructions about who to kill and who to preserve. So basically all the Solomon's opposition (anyone supporting his older brother, Adonijah, the expected heir to the throne) is eliminated and thus his kingdom "firmly established." Ascending to and maintaining power for kings was a difficult and bloody business and David and Solomon are no exception. Say good-bye to Joab who, ever loyal to David, probably took matters into his own hands one too many times. Also, David never forgave him for killing Absalom.

1st Kings 8

Solomon's Prayer

[22] Then Solomon stood before the altar of the LORD in the presence of all the assembly of Israel, and spread out his
hands to heaven. [23] He said, "O LORD, God of Israel, there is no God like you in heaven above or on earth beneath,
keeping covenant and steadfast love for your servants who walk before you with all their heart, [24] the covenant that
you kept for your servant my father David as you declared to him; you promised with your mouth and have this day
fulfilled with your hand. [....] [41] "Likewise when a foreigner, who is not of your people Israel, comes from a distant land
because of your name [42] --for they shall hear of your great name, your mighty hand, and your outstretched arm--when
a foreigner comes and prays toward this house, [43] then hear in heaven your dwelling place, and do according to all that
the foreigner calls to you, so that all the peoples of the earth may know your name and fear you, as do your people
Israel, and so that they may know that your name has been invoked on this house that I have built.

Now that I've Killed Off All My Brothers

Musings

Under Solomon God upgrades from a tent into a full-up, no-holds-barred, big deal, uptown, temple. David wanted to build it, but God via Nathan told him to wait for Solomon to do it. In this passage an excerpt of a fairly long and involved temple dedication is underway. Basically Solomon reminds God of the covenant to Israel and to David. It's probably not uncommon to want to remind God of the deal they have, yet one has to wonder how unnecessary it really is. Perhaps it's more to remind the people who hear the prayer than to remind God. It may be like saying to the nation of Israel "hey look guys, we have this deal with God, live up to it ... and by the way God chose you, this temple and David and thereby me ... so honor it."

1st Kings 17:8-16

The Prophet Relocation Program

[8] Then the word of the LORD came to him [Elijah], saying, [9] "Go now to Zarephath, which belongs to Sidon, and live there; for I have commanded a widow there to feed you." [10] So he set out and went to Zarephath. When he came to the gate of the town, a widow was there gathering sticks; he called to her and said, "Bring me a little water in a vessel, so that I may drink." [11] As she was going to bring it, he called to her and said, "Bring me a morsel of bread in your hand." [12] But she said, "As the LORD your God lives, I have nothing baked, only a handful of meal in a jar, and a little oil in a jug; I am now gathering a couple of sticks, so that I may go home and prepare it for myself and my son, that we may eat it, and die." [13] Elijah said to her, "Do not be afraid; go and do as you have said; but first make me a little cake of it and bring it to me, and afterwards make something for yourself and your son. [14] For thus says the LORD the God of Israel: The jar of meal will not be emptied and the jug of oil will not fail until the day that the LORD sends rain on the earth." [15] She went and did as Elijah said, so that she as well as he and her household ate for many days. [16] The jar of meal was not emptied, neither did the jug of oil fail, according to the word of the LORD that he spoke by Elijah.

Old Mother Hubbard

Musings

Solomon reigns for 40 years, as did David, but once he passes, the northern tribes secede splitting the nation back into Israel (Northern kingdom) and Judah (Southern kingdom). At this point in the story of the prophet Elijah (whose name means *My God is the LORD*) begins. Elijah is strongly opposed to King Ahab (Israel's king) and Jezebel, Ahab's Baal worshipping wife, because of his lack of regard for the God of Israel. Just prior to this passage, Elijah announces a drought which comes to pass as a sort of "in your face" to Baal, the god of the storm and rain. Elijah is directed to go to this widow in Zarephath where God provides them with food. This is smack in the center of Phoenician Baal worship, so it is no accident. Elijah will be in the middle of things and God is in control.

1st Kings 17:17-24

Elijah Revives the Widow's Son

*[17] After this the son of the woman, the mistress of the house, became ill; his illness was so severe that there was no
breath left in him. [18] She then said to Elijah, "What have you against me, O man of God? You have come to me to bring
my sin to remembrance, and to cause the death of my son!" [19] But he said to her, "Give me your son." He took him from
her bosom, carried him up into the upper chamber where he was lodging, and laid him on his own bed. [20] He cried out
to the LORD, "O LORD my God, have you brought calamity even upon the widow with whom I am staying, by killing
her son?" [21] Then he stretched himself upon the child three times, and cried out to the LORD, "O LORD my God, let this
child's life come into him again." [22] The LORD listened to the voice of Elijah; the life of the child came into him again,
and he revived. [23] Elijah took the child, brought him down from the upper chamber into the house, and gave him to his
mother; then Elijah said, "See, your son is alive." [24] So the woman said to Elijah, "Now I know that you are a man of
God, and that the word of the LORD in your mouth is truth."*

Widow Retirement Bail-Out

Musings

The widow is afraid that the very presence of Elijah in her household has alerted God to her sins, and that her son's death was the result. This really isn't the case, but it provides a way to show just how much God is speaking through Elijah and that faith in God trumps even death. The son's life is restored, the widow's faith is renewed and Elijah's relationship with YHWH (the LORD, God) is clearly established. There are probably more cakes in the deal for Elijah, if I had to guess.

1st Kings 19:1-8
Jezebel's Threat

Ahab told Jezebel all that Elijah had done, and how he had killed all the prophets with the sword. 2 Then Jezebel sent
a messenger to Elijah, saying, "So may the gods do to me, and more also, if I do not make your life like the life of one
of them by this time tomorrow." 3 Then he was afraid; he got up and fled for his life, and came to Beer-sheba, which
belongs to Judah; he left his servant there. 4 But he himself went a day's journey into the wilderness, and came and sat
down under a solitary broom tree. He asked that he might die: "It is enough; now, O LORD, take away my life, for I
am no better than my ancestors." 5 Then he lay down under the broom tree and fell asleep. Suddenly an angel touched
him and said to him, "Get up and eat." 6 He looked, and there at his head was a cake baked on hot stones, and a jar of
water. He ate and drank, and lay down again. 7 The angel of the LORD came a second time, touched him, and said,
"Get up and eat, otherwise the journey will be too much for you." 8 He got up, and ate and drank; then he went in the
strength of that food forty days and forty nights to Horeb the mount of God.

God 1, Baal 0

Musings

Elijah had just finished challenging Ahab and the priests of Baal to a fire building contest. Not only did the priests lose, but they were all killed. Coincidently the drought ends. Now Jezebel hears of this and swears revenge, to which Elijah flees to the Southern most part of Judah. He seems pretty shaken by the threat and figures he had done his job, discrediting Baal worship, and his usefulness to God is done. However, God provides more yummy cakes and has him go on a 40 day journey to Mt. Horeb (Northern kingdom's name for Mt. Sinai) thus back in the Northern kingdom. The 40 days and Sinai connection probably serve to connect Elijah to Moses as a great prophet of the LORD.

1st Kings 19:9-14

Epiphany for Elijah

9 At that place he came to a cave, and spent the night there. Then the word of the LORD came to him, saying, "What
are you doing here, Elijah?" 10 He answered, "I have been very zealous for the LORD, the God of hosts; for the Israel-
ites have forsaken your covenant, thrown down your altars, and killed your prophets with the sword. I alone am left,
and they are seeking my life, to take it away." 11 He said, "Go out and stand on the mountain before the LORD, for the
LORD is about to pass by." Now there was a great wind, so strong that it was splitting mountains and breaking rocks
in pieces before the LORD, but the LORD was not in the wind; and after the wind an earthquake, but the LORD was
not in the earthquake; 12 and after the earthquake a fire, but the LORD was not in the fire; and after the fire a sound of
sheer silence. 13 When Elijah heard it, he wrapped his face in his mantle and went out and stood at the entrance of the
cave. Then there came a voice to him that said, "What are you doing here, Elijah?" 14 He answered, "I have been very
zealous for the LORD, the God of hosts; for the Israelites have forsaken your covenant, thrown down your altars, and
killed your prophets with the sword. I alone am left, and they are seeking my life, to take it away."

Who's That Knocking at My Door?

Musings

It's clear that Elijah still isn't quite up-to-speed with God's plan at this point. On Mt. Sinai (Horeb) Elijah is still hiding out in a cave. What happens next is a theophany (appearance of God), and yet a very unexpected one. God does not appear in the wind, earthquake nor fire, but in a whisper out of the sheer silence. Elijah covers his face (per Moses) and prepares to be addressed by God in the very presence of God. It starts with the question ... "what are you doing here!?" Elijah is sticking with his story, but is God buying it?

1st Kings 19:15-21

God's Plan for Elijah

15 Then the LORD said to him, "Go, return on your way to the wilderness of Damascus; when you arrive, you shall
anoint Hazael as king over Aram. 16 Also you shall anoint Jehu son of Nimshi as king over Israel; and you shall anoint
Elisha son of Shaphat of Abel-meholah as prophet in your place. 17 Whoever escapes from the sword of Hazael, Jehu
shall kill; and whoever escapes from the sword of Jehu, Elisha shall kill. 18 Yet I will leave seven thousand in Israel, all
the knees that have not bowed to Baal, and every mouth that has not kissed him." 19 So he set out from there, and found
Elisha son of Shaphat, who was plowing. There were twelve yoke of oxen ahead of him, and he was with the twelfth.
Elijah passed by him and threw his mantle over him. 20 He left the oxen, ran after Elijah, and said, "Let me kiss my
father and my mother, and then I will follow you." Then Elijah said to him, "Go back again; for what have I done to
you?" 21 He returned from following him, took the yoke of oxen, and slaughtered them; using the equipment from the
oxen, he boiled their flesh, and gave it to the people, and they ate. Then he set out and followed Elijah, and became
his servant.

Directions Not Included

Musings

What Elijah hears must be music to his ears. He gets to appoint two kings, one of which, Jehu, will supplant Ahab as well as name a successor in Elisha. Seven thousand Israelites have remained loyal to God (or at least not worshipped Baal) and will be the new start for the Northern kingdom. Elisha is selected to be Elijah's disciple and later his successor. Elisha asks to be allowed to say good-bye to his old life and Elijah seems to give him permission to do so. Of course the mantle Elijah really throws onto Elisha is not a fireplace mantle, but rather an outer robe or cloak that symbolizes the owner. Elijah giving it to Elisha is sort of a "what's mine is yours" moment.

1st Kings 21

Elijah and Ahab Meet at Last

Later the following events took place: Naboth the Jezreelite had a vineyard in Jezreel, beside the palace of King Ahab of Samaria. [2] And Ahab said to Naboth, "Give me your vineyard, so that I may have it for a vegetable garden, because it is near my house; I will give you a better vineyard for it; or, if it seems good to you, I will give you its value in money." [...] [17] Then the word of the LORD came to Elijah the Tishbite, saying: [18] Go down to meet King Ahab of Israel, who rules in Samaria; he is now in the vineyard of Naboth, where he has gone to take possession. [19] You shall say to him, "Thus says the LORD: Have you killed, and also taken possession?" You shall say to him, "Thus says the LORD: In the place where dogs licked up the blood of Naboth, dogs will also lick up your blood." [20] Ahab said to Elijah, "Have you found me, O my enemy?" He answered, "I have found you. Because you have sold yourself to do what is evil in the sight of the LORD, [21] I will bring disaster on you; I will consume you, and will cut off from Ahab every male, bond or free, in Israel; [22] and I will make your house like the house of Jeroboam son of Nebat, and like the house of Baasha son of Ahijah, because you have provoked me to anger and have caused Israel to sin.

Thar She Blows

Musings

What's missing are the verses where Jezebel conspires to have Naboth killed so Ahab may take his vineyard. At any rate, the plot is uncovered, Elijah has a movie-like redeeming, climatic moment where he confronts Ahab to tell him it's over. He lays it all out for him and it isn't pretty. The sweetness of the victory is delayed however. Immediately after this confrontation (and passage) Ahab repents. He is allowed to live and his fate will be carried out at his death rather than right then and there. Nothing more is said of Jezebel nor Elijah in 1st Kings, but God and Elijah have made their point.

2nd Kings

2nd Kings 2

Passing the Mantle

Now when the LORD was about to take Elijah up to heaven by a whirlwind, Elijah and Elisha were on their way from Gilgal. 2
Elijah said to Elisha, "Stay here; for the LORD has sent me as far as Bethel." But Elisha said, "As the LORD lives, and as you your-
self live, I will not leave you." So they went down to Bethel. 3 The company of prophets who were in Bethel came out to Elisha, and
said to him, "Do you know that today the LORD will take your master away from you?" And he said, "Yes, I know; keep silent."
4 Elijah said to him, "Elisha, stay here; for the LORD has sent me to Jericho." But he said, "As the LORD lives, and as you yourself
live, I will not leave you." So they came to Jericho. 5 The company of prophets who were at Jericho drew near to Elisha, and said
to him, "Do you know that today the LORD will take your master away from you?" And he answered, "Yes, I know; be silent." 6
Then Elijah said to him, "Stay here; for the LORD has sent me to the Jordan." But he said, "As the LORD lives, and as you your-
self live, I will not leave you." So the two of
them went on. 7 Fifty men of the company of
prophets also went, and stood at some dis-
tance from them, as they both were standing
by the Jordan. 8 Then Elijah took his mantle
and rolled it up, and struck the water; the
water was parted to the one side and to
the other, until the two of them crossed on
dry ground. 9 When they had crossed, Eli-
jah said to Elisha, "Tell me what I may do
for you, before I am taken from you." Elisha
said, "Please let me inherit a double share
of your spirit." 10 He responded, "You have
asked a hard thing; yet, if you see me as I
am being taken from you, it will be granted
you; if not, it will not." 11 As they continued
walking and talking, a chariot of fire and
horses of fire separated the two of them, and
Elijah ascended in a whirlwind into heav-
en. 12 Elisha kept watching and crying out,
"Father, father! The chariots of Israel and
its horsemen!" But when he could no lon-
ger see him, he grasped his own clothes and
tore them in two pieces. 13 He picked up the
mantle of Elijah that had fallen from him,
and went back and stood on the bank of the
Jordan. 14 He took the mantle of Elijah that
had fallen from him, and struck the water,
saying, "Where is the LORD, the God of Elijah?" When he had struck the water, the water was parted to the one side and to the
other, and Elisha went over.

Passing the Mantle

Musings

This is literally where Elijah passes the mantle to Elisha, or God does anyway. Elisha is a loyal disciple and servant to Elijah and will not part from him until he has absolutely no choice. Elijah parting the Jordan with his mantle (cloak not fireplace shelf) rolled up like a staff is a direct symbolic link (again) to Moses. By Elisha asking for a double portion from Elijah, he is asking for a first-born son's share of an inheritance. Elijah doesn't grant or refuse this request, but later God grants it. Elisha comes back and parts the Jordan demonstrating that he is now officially Elijah's successor. The fifty disciples serve as a witness. Chariots, whirlwinds, horsemen, fire are all common symbols of God appearing (theophany), also evidence of the spectacular exit Elijah was granted. Perhaps one of the more elaborate retirement ceremonies in the Old Testament and inspiring at least one very well-known song (Swing Low Sweet Chariot).

2nd Kings 4

No Good Deed Goes Unpunished

*8 One day Elisha was passing through Shunem, where a wealthy woman lived, who urged him to have a meal. So
whenever he passed that way, he would stop there for a meal. 9 She said to her husband, "Look, I am sure that this man
who regularly passes our way is a holy man of God. 10 Let us make a small roof chamber with walls, and put there for
him a bed, a table, a chair, and a lamp, so that he can stay there whenever he comes to us." 11 One day when he came
there, he went up to the chamber and lay down there. 12 He said to his servant Gehazi, "Call the Shunammite woman."
When he had called her, she stood before him. 13 He said to him, "Say to her, Since you have taken all this trouble for
us, what may be done for you? Would you have a word spoken on your behalf to the king or to the commander of the
army?" She answered, "I live among my own people." 14 He said, "What then may be done for her?" Gehazi answered,
"Well, she has no son, and her husband is old." 15 He said, "Call her." When he had called her, she stood at the door. 16
He said, "At this season, in due time, you shall embrace a son." She replied, "No, my lord, O man of God; do not deceive
your servant." 17 The woman conceived and bore a son at that season, in due time, as Elisha had declared to her.*

Roomatism

Musings

Elisha performs many miracles along the lines of Elijah, and this is no exception. The only hint of why the Shunammite woman wanted a child was because her husband was old. This could be anything from needing an heir to help in managing the family business to simply the desire to have children. In this case the man and woman are wealthy, so they don't need children to see to their care in old age, but in most other cases that would be a good bet. There was no retirement system per se back in the day. God is often associated with fertility or lack there of, so the request would not be considered out of the ordinary. God, through Elisha, grants the request.

2nd Kings 5

Naaman Soaks His Head

Naaman, commander of the army of the king of Aram, was a great man and in high favor with his master, because by him the
LORD had given victory to Aram. The man, though a mighty warrior, suffered from leprosy. 2 Now the Arameans on one of their
raids had taken a young girl captive from the land of Israel, and she served Naaman's wife. 3 She said to her mistress, "If only my
lord were with the prophet who is in Samaria! He would cure him of his leprosy." 4 So Naaman went in and told his lord just what
the girl from the land of Israel had said. 5 And the king of Aram said, "Go then, and I will send along a letter to the king of Israel."
He went, taking with him ten talents of silver, six thousand shekels of gold, and ten sets of garments. 6 He brought the letter to the
king of Israel, which read, "When this letter reaches you, know that I have sent to you my servant Naaman, that you may cure
him of his leprosy." 7 When the king of Israel read the letter, he tore his clothes and said, "Am I God, to give death or life, that this
man sends word to me to cure a man of his leprosy? Just look and see how he is trying to pick a quarrel with me." 8 But when Elisha
the man of God heard that the king
of Israel had torn his clothes, he
sent a message to the king, "Why
have you torn your clothes? Let
him come to me, that he may learn
that there is a prophet in Israel." 9
So Naaman came with his horses
and chariots, and halted at the
entrance of Elisha's house. 10 Eli-
sha sent a messenger to him, say-
ing, "Go, wash in the Jordan seven
times, and your flesh shall be re-
stored and you shall be clean." 11
But Naaman became angry and
went away, saying, "I thought that
for me he would surely come out,
and stand and call on the name
of the LORD his God, and would
wave his hand over the spot, and
cure the leprosy! 12 Are not Abana
and Pharpar, the rivers of Damas-
cus, better than all the waters of
Israel? Could I not wash in them,
and be clean?" He turned and
went away in a rage. 13 But his ser-
vants approached and said to him,
"Father, if the prophet had com-
manded you to do something dif-
ficult, would you not have done it?
How much more, when all he said
to you was, 'Wash, and be clean'?"
14 So he went down and immersed himself seven times in the Jordan, according to the word of the man of God; his flesh was re-
stored like the flesh of a young boy, and he was clean.

Go Soak Your Head

Musings

The LORD (YHWH) is already responsible for Naaman's military victories, although he probably isn't aware of it. As noted earlier, God is seen as being in control of all events regardless of which side wins. Elisha basically messes with Naaman's giant ego, but eventually he does as Elisha instructs, and the wise servant urges, and is cleansed of his leprosy. Reading on through verses 15-19 (grab a Bible) he also converts and believes in the LORD. The good news is two-fold, 1) Naaman is cured of his ego and leprosy and gains true faith, and 2) God is shown as healing even a non-Israelite willing to ask for help.

2nd Kings 13

What We Have Here is a Failure to Communicate

*14 Now when Elisha had fallen sick with the illness of which he was to die, King Joash of Israel went down to him, and
wept before him, crying, "My father, my father! The chariots of Israel and its horsemen!" 15 Elisha said to him, "Take a
bow and arrows"; so he took a bow and arrows. 16 Then he said to the king of Israel, "Draw the bow"; and he drew it.
Elisha laid his hands on the king's hands. 17 Then he said, "Open the window eastward"; and he opened it. Elisha said,
"Shoot"; and he shot. Then he said, "The Lord's arrow of victory, the arrow of victory over Aram! For you shall fight
the Arameans in Aphek until you have made an end of them." 18 He continued, "Take the arrows"; and he took them.
He said to the king of Israel, "Strike the ground with them"; he struck three times, and stopped. 19 Then the man of God
was angry with him, and said, "You should have struck five or six times; then you would have struck down Aram until
you had made an end of it, but now you will strike down Aram only three times." 20 So Elisha died, and they buried
him. Now bands of Moabites used to invade the land in the spring of the year.*

Knock 3 Times on the Ceiling If You Love Me

Musings

Elisha is a prophet for 60 years and is quite old now. Joash comes to visit needing a blessing for a military win over Aram. He receives one, but only partially. Apparently Elisha did not like the fact that Joash only struck the ground three times and therefore he would only win 3 victories over Aram. He needed more victories than that for total victory, but it is at least something. Elisha then dies, not in a spectacular show as Elijah's exit, but simply passes and is buried somewhere. It was a long and successful tenure for the prophet to say the least.

2nd Chronicles

2nd Chronicles 36

Bad King, Good King

[14] All the leading priests and the people also were exceedingly unfaithful, following all the abominations of the nations; and
they polluted the house of the LORD that he had consecrated in Jerusalem. [15] The LORD, the God of their ancestors, sent
persistently to them by his messengers, because he had compassion on his people and on his dwelling place; [16] but they kept
mocking the messengers of God, despising his words, and scoffing at his prophets, until the wrath of the LORD against his
people became so great that there was no remedy. [17] Therefore he brought up against them the king of the Chaldeans, who
killed their youths with the sword in the house of their sanctuary, and had no compassion on young man or young woman, the
aged or the feeble; he gave them
all into his hand. [18] All the ves-
sels of the house of God, large
and small, and the treasures of
the house of the LORD, and the
treasures of the king and of his
officials, all these he brought
to Babylon. [19] They burned the
house of God, broke down the
wall of Jerusalem, burned all its
palaces with fire, and destroyed
all its precious vessels. [20] He took
into exile in Babylon those who
had escaped from the sword, and
they became servants to him and
to his sons until the establish-
ment of the kingdom of Persia,
[21] to fulfill the word of the LORD
by the mouth of Jeremiah, un-
til the land had made up for its
sabbaths. All the days that it lay
desolate it kept sabbath, to fulfill
seventy years. [22] In the first year
of King Cyrus of Persia, in fulfill-
ment of the word of the LORD
spoken by Jeremiah, the LORD
stirred up the spirit of King Cyrus
of Persia so that he sent a herald
throughout all his kingdom and
also declared in a written edict:
[23] "Thus says King Cyrus of Persia: The LORD, the God of heaven, has given me all the kingdoms of the earth, and he has
charged me to build him a house at Jerusalem, which is in Judah. Whoever is among you of all his people, may the LORD
his God be with him! Let him go up."

Jeremiah's "I Told You So" Moment

Musings

The reason the LORD used the king of the Chaldeans to destroy Judah was because they refused to repent, not because they had sinned. It's one thing to make mistakes and quite another to be belligerent about them once exposed. According to Chronicles, God acts through foreign kings to bring about a sort of retributive justice. After 70 years God again acts through a foreign king, King Cyrus of Persia, to restore Jerusalem and the temple. The book of Kings has the temple being ravaged, but in Chronicles it was totally destroyed. The task of rebuilding would be difficult and take many years, since Jerusalem and the temple were in ruins. This was both an opportunity and a huge challenge.

Nehemiah

Nehemiah 8

The First Law School

All the people gathered together into the square before the Water Gate. They told the scribe Ezra to bring the book of the law of Moses, which the LORD had given to Israel. 2 Accordingly, the priest Ezra brought the law before the assembly, both men and women and all who could hear with understanding. This was on the first day of the seventh month. 3 He read from it facing the square before the Water Gate from early morning until midday, in the presence of the men and the women and those who could understand; and the ears of all the people were attentive to the book of the law. 4 The scribe Ezra stood on a wooden platform that had been made for the purpose; and beside him stood Mattithiah, Shema, Anaiah, Uriah, Hilkiah, and Maaseiah on his right hand; and Pedaiah, Mishael, Malchijah, Hashum, Hash-baddanah, Zechariah, and Meshullam on his left hand. 5 And Ezra opened the book in the sight of all the people, for he was standing above all the people; and when he opened it, all the people stood up. 6 Then Ezra blessed the LORD, the great God, and all the people answered, "Amen, Amen," lifting up their hands. Then they bowed their heads and worshiped the LORD with their faces to the ground. 7 Also Jeshua, Bani, Sherebiah, Jamin, Akkub, Shabbethai, Hodiah, Maaseiah, Kelita, Azariah, Jozabad, Hanan, Pelaiah, the Levites, helped the people to understand the law, while the people remained in their places. 8 So they read from the book, from the law of God, with interpretation. They gave the sense, so that the people understood the reading. 9 And Nehemiah, who was the governor, and Ezra the priest and scribe, and the Levites who taught the people said to all the people, "This day is holy to the LORD your God; do not mourn or weep." For all the people wept when they heard the words of the law. 10 Then he said to them, "Go your way, eat the fat and drink sweet wine and send portions of them to those for whom nothing is prepared, for this day is holy to our LORD; and do not be grieved, for the joy of the LORD is your strength."

It's All Greek to Me

Musings

Nehemiah is the leader tasked with rebuilding Jerusalem and the temple and Ezra is his chief priest. The books of Ezra and Nehemiah may have originally been one volume and are sort of memoirs to them. Here a major wall has been restored and Ezra uses the occasion of the dedication and celebration to remind Israel of the law. It's hard to imagine what he could have done to make six hours of reading from the law interesting, but apparently it was very well-received and the party afterwards may have been worth the wait. The difficulty of restoring the city should not be underestimated, in addition to relocating back to a city that was essentially in ruins. It would take many decades to restore it.

Job

Job 7

No Good Deed Will Go Unpunished

"Do not human beings have a hard service on earth, and are not their days like the days of a laborer? 2 Like a slave
who longs for the shadow, and like laborers who look for their wages, 3 so I am allotted months of emptiness, and nights
of misery are apportioned to me. 4 When I lie down I say, 'When shall I rise?' But the night is long, and I am full of
tossing until dawn. 5 My flesh is clothed with worms and dirt; my skin hardens, then breaks out again. 6 My days are
swifter than a weaver's shuttle, and come to their end without hope. 7 "Remember that my life is a breath; my eye will
never again see good."

So You Had a Bad Day

Musings

The book of Job is a magnificent work of prose and poetry basically dealing with the complex question of why bad things happen to good people. It tends to refute the prevailing conventional wisdom while at the same time never giving a direct answer to the questions it raises. If you want to be challenged and amazed, pick up a good study Bible or commentary on Job and dig into it in-depth. The few passages covered by the lectionary only scratch the surface. In this passage we see that Job is in the midst of suffering. Satan, acting as a prosecuting attorney, is basically challenging God's faith and humanity (through Job), suggesting only those that are well-off will praise God. It's noteworthy to realize that Satan is acting within God's court, not in opposition to it. Job is caught in the middle of this argument and becomes the test case (or guinea pig) to see just how far you have to push humanity before they renounce God. It's fairly clear that being the test case is not a good thing.

Job 28

The Search for Wisdom Continues

"Surely there is a mine for silver, and a place for gold to be refined. 2 Iron is taken out of the earth, and copper is smelted from ore. 3 Miners put an end to darkness, and search out to the farthest bound the ore in gloom and deep darkness. 4 They open shafts in a valley away from human habitation; they are forgotten by travelers, they sway suspended, remote from people. 5 As for the earth, out of it comes bread; but underneath it is turned up as by fire. 6 Its stones are the place of sapphires, and its dust contains gold. 7 "That path no bird of prey knows, and the falcon's eye has not seen it. 8 The proud wild animals have not trodden it; the lion has not passed over it. 9 "They put their hand to the flinty rock, and overturn mountains by the roots. 10 They cut out channels in the rocks, and their eyes see every precious thing. 11 The sources of the rivers they probe; hidden things they bring to light. 12 "But where shall wisdom be found? And where is the place of understanding? 13 Mortals do not know the way to it, and it is not found in the land of the living. 14 The deep says, 'It is not in me,' and the sea says, 'It is not with me.' 15 It cannot be gotten for gold, and silver cannot be weighed out as its price. 16 It cannot be valued in the gold of Ophir, in precious onyx or sapphire. 17 Gold and glass cannot equal it, nor can it be exchanged for jewels of fine gold. 18 No mention shall be made of coral or of crystal; the price of wisdom is above pearls. 19 The chrysolite of Ethiopia cannot compare with it, nor can it be valued in pure gold. 20 "Where then does wisdom come from? And where is the place of understanding? 21 It is hidden from the eyes of all living, and concealed from the birds of the air. 22 Abaddon and Death say, 'We have heard a rumor of it with our ears.' 23 "God understands the way to it, and he knows its place. 24 For he looks to the ends of the earth, and sees everything under the heavens. 25 When he gave to the wind its weight, and apportioned out the waters by measure; 26 when he made a decree for the rain, and a way for the thunderbolt; 27 then he saw it and declared it; he established it, and searched it out. 28 And he said to humankind, 'Truly, the fear of the Lord, that is wisdom; and to depart from evil is understanding.'"

Looking for Wisdom in All the Wrong Places

Musings

This poetic interlude is a tribute to wisdom. The central questions are emphasized in verses 12 and 20 which basically ask how to attain wisdom. It suggests that man is so smart as to being almost godlike compared to animals but, even so, is still barely able to scratch the surface of the wisdom of God. Ecclesiastes would be proud.

Job 42

Say What?

Then Job answered the LORD: [2] "I know that you can do all things, and that no purpose of yours can be thwarted. [3] 'Who is this that hides counsel without knowledge?' Therefore I have uttered what I did not understand, things too wonderful for me, which I did not know. [4] 'Hear, and I will speak; I will question you, and you declare to me.' [5] I had heard of you by the hearing of the ear, but now my eye sees you; [6] therefore I despise myself, and repent in dust and ashes."

Got Wind?

Musings

Job has just been in dialogue with God about his condition. God provides a very definitive non-answer to his question (chapter 41), leaving Job to this response above. Job is essentially saying that he now realizes God is not going to answer his questions, so he is reluctantly giving up. After this encounter however, Job is more than restored to his former good condition and in most respects he passed the test (held to his faith and did not renounce God). Of course, his original wife, family and cattle probably weren't too thrilled by the test. It's similar to an action-adventure movie; it never pays to be the best friend of the hero.

Proverbs

Proverbs 2

Hidden Treasure

My child, if you accept my words and treasure up my commandments within you, 2 making your ear attentive to wis-
dom and inclining your heart to understanding; 3 if you indeed cry out for insight, and raise your voice for understand-
ing; 4 if you seek it like silver, and search for it as for hidden treasures-- 5 then you will understand the fear of the LORD
and find the knowledge of God. 6 For the LORD gives wisdom; from his mouth come knowledge and understanding; 7
he stores up sound wisdom for the upright; he is a shield to those who walk blamelessly, 8 guarding the paths of justice
and preserving the way of his faithful ones.

Digging Up the Word of God

Musings

Proverbs is a book full of instructions and guidelines aimed at building character. Proverbs, Ecclesiastes and Job are considered the wisdom books of the Old Testament (along with Sirach and the Wisdom of Solomon in the Apocrypha). None is probably more fun and approachable than Proverbs in that it is full of advice and sayings, none of which are meant as universal commands, but rather are contextual guidelines aimed at teaching how to discern the proper things to do and how to live well. This passage basically says that wisdom can be sought and found and should be valued above all else. Not exactly booty, but a guide to a life well-lived. So while Job and Ecclesiastes sort of take the negative route emphasizing our inability to grasp the full wisdom of God, Proverbs provides a path to the things we should be able to figure out, if we are willing to work at it.

Proverbs 8

Wise Beyond Your Years

22 The LORD created me at the beginning of his work, the first of his acts of long ago. 23 Ages ago I was set up, at the
first, before the beginning of the earth. 24 When there were no depths I was brought forth, when there were no springs
abounding with water. 25 Before the mountains had been shaped, before the hills, I was brought forth-- 26 when he had
not yet made earth and fields, or the world's first bits of soil. 27 When he established the heavens, I was there, when he
drew a circle on the face of the deep, 28 when he made firm the skies above, when he established the fountains of the
deep, 29 when he assigned to the sea its limit, so that the waters might not transgress his command, when he marked
out the foundations of the earth, 30 then I was beside him, like a master worker; and I was daily his delight, rejoicing
before him always, 31 rejoicing in his inhabited world and delighting in the human race.

Older than the Hills

Musings

This is a piece of the longest single description of wisdom in the Bible (verses 1-36). This part of the description discusses wisdom's role in creation. The underlying difficulty, in my opinion, is that wisdom has no role outside of human behavior (the last part of creation), except to say that was the first thing God was concerned with. Humans, since they can reason, are the only animals on the planet that would be concerned with right and wrong (hence morality). That aside, this is more to show the primacy of wisdom in the scheme of things. Anyone looking at the natural order should be able to see God clearly manifest in it. In a sense wisdom was God's best friend, like a dog always at God's side enjoying all that was taking place.

Proverbs 22

Priceless

A good name is to be chosen rather than great riches, and favor is better than silver or gold. [2] *The rich and the poor have this in common: the LORD is the maker of them all.* [3] *The clever see danger and hide; but the simple go on, and suffer for it.* [4] *The reward for humility and fear of the LORD is riches and honor and life.* [5] *Thorns and snares are in the way of the perverse; the cautious will keep far from them.* [6] *Train children in the right way, and when old, they will not stray.* [7] *The rich rules over the poor, and the borrower is the slave of the lender.* [8] *Whoever sows injustice will reap calamity, and the rod of anger will fail.* [9] *Those who are generous are blessed, for they share their bread with the poor.*

What's In Your Wallet?

Musings

Well, this is clearly a nice set of ideals, simply stated and perhaps true on a good day. Job might take issue with this at various points of his test, but may generally agree with it afterwards. Still, all-in-all it's a good set of guidelines - live right, stay way from bad people, raise your kids right, and be generous and care for the poor. In the words of Mr. Spock - live long and prosper.

<u>Side note</u>: the next book in the Bible is another wisdom book - Ecclesiastes. This is one of my favorite books in the Old Testament and is well worth the twelve very short chapters to read. It's not mentioned in the lectionary so it won't be addressed in this book but it ponders the meaning of life in an interesting way.

Isaiah

Isaiah 2

God's Place

The word that Isaiah son of Amoz saw concerning Judah and Jerusalem. [2] In days to come the mountain of the Lord's house shall be established as the highest of the mountains, and shall be raised above the hills; all the nations shall stream to it. [3] Many peoples shall come and say, "Come, let us go up to the mountain of the LORD, to the house of the God of Jacob; that he may teach us his ways and that we may walk in his paths." For out of Zion shall go forth instruction, and the word of the LORD from Jerusalem. [4] He shall judge between the nations, and shall arbitrate for many peoples; they shall beat their swords into plowshares, and their spears into pruning hooks; nation shall not lift up sword against nation, neither shall they learn war any more. [5] O house of Jacob, come, let us walk in the light of the LORD!

Peace in the Valley

Musings

Looking toward the future, Isaiah sees Jerusalem as God's central governing point for all the nations and where peace has been established. Zion is used here as another name for Jerusalem emphasizing it's pivotal role for God and humanity. Verse 4, beating swords into plowshares is a well-known passage from Isaiah often used as a description of a utopian society where there is no longer any need for weapons.

Isaiah 6

What Have You Been Smoking?

In the year that King Uzziah died, I saw the Lord sitting on a throne, high and lofty; and the hem of his robe filled the temple. [2] Seraphs were in attendance above him; each had six wings: with two they covered their faces, and with two they covered their feet, and with two they flew. [3] And one called to another and said: "Holy, holy, holy is the LORD of hosts; the whole earth is full of his glory." [4] The pivots on the thresholds shook at the voices of those who called, and the house filled with smoke. [5] And I said: "Woe is me! I am lost, for I am a man of unclean lips, and I live among a people of unclean lips; yet my eyes have seen the King, the LORD of hosts!" [6] Then one of the seraphs flew to me, holding a live coal that had been taken from the altar with a pair of tongs. [7] The seraph touched my mouth with it and said: "Now that this has touched your lips, your guilt has departed and your sin is blotted out." [8] Then I heard the voice of the Lord saying, "Whom shall I send, and who will go for us?" And I said, "Here am I; send me!"

Hors D'oeuvres Anyone

Musings

This is Isaiah's calling story. He is unworthy to be a prophet until the seraph touched a hot coal to his mouth, purifying him for the task to come (aka being a prophet). Isaiah gives a familiar prophet response, "here am I," to the Lord's call.

Isaiah 7

The Calming of the King

10 Again the LORD spoke to Ahaz, saying, 11 Ask a sign of the LORD your God; let it be deep as Sheol or high as heaven.
12 But Ahaz said, I will not ask, and I will not put the LORD to the test. 13 Then Isaiah said: "Hear then, O house of
David! Is it too little for you to weary mortals, that you weary my God also? 14 Therefore the Lord himself will give you
a sign. Look, the young woman is with child and shall bear a son, and shall name him Immanuel. 15 He shall eat curds
and honey by the time he knows how to refuse the evil and choose the good.

Breakfast of Champions

Musings

This passage is unintelligible by itself which is the danger of taking passages out of context. Basically it is in the middle (reinforcement to earlier warnings) of Isaiah warning king Ahaz not to align with the Assyrians. Ahaz seems to be humble not wanting to put God to the test but what he's really saying is that he doesn't want God to give him a sign contrary to his desire to make the alliance. You could relate this to being a kid facing the choice of asking your mom for a cookie when you know the answer will be no, or not asking so that you can do what you want. Isaiah is basically saying, you're not going to ask, but God is going to give you a sign anyway and it will be a son who will be called Immanuel (God is with us). In other words, God will be with your son (or possibly Isaiah's son), but not necessarily with you. The finer things of life, like curds and honey, will come to Judah under him (and possibly not Ahaz if he doesn't listen to God). At this point Assyria is threatening Israel, and Judah and Israel are also sort of in a civil war. Over time Assyria will conquer Israel, and Judah will become a vassal state paying tribute to Assyria, but for now Isaiah wants Judah to remain independent and not ally with Assyria. Isaiah probably views it as selling out part of their own people even though Israel and Judah are separate kingdoms.

Isaiah 9

Is it Reigning Out?

But there will be no gloom for those who were in anguish. In the former time he brought into contempt the land of Zebulun and the land of Naphtali, but in the latter time he will make glorious the way of the sea, the land beyond the Jordan, Galilee of the nations. [2] The people who walked in darkness have seen a great light; those who lived in a land of deep darkness-- on them light has shined. [3] You have multiplied the nation, you have increased its joy; they rejoice before you as with joy at the harvest, as people exult when dividing plunder. [4] For the yoke of their burden, and the bar across their shoulders, the rod of their oppressor, you have broken as on the day of Midian.

Light at the End of the Tunnel

Musings

Isaiah is probably referring to king Hezekiah whom he hopes will reunite Israel and Judah again. It doesn't quite work out as planned thanks to Assyria (and obviously Israel wasn't too interested in uniting with Judah at the time anyway). Isaiah envisions a united Israel with a king in the lineage of David. When Israel split from Judah, the 10 northern tribes' kings were not davidic, while Judah maintained the davidic line. This was often used by Judah as part of its claim to legitimacy over Israel. This is later used in Christianity as part of the argument to legitimize messianic kingship and partly why Isaiah is often quoted or referenced in the New Testament (and represents about 20% of the Old Testament lectionary passages). At any rate, it is here a mixed message of hope and warning ... hope for a united kingdom at some point in the future, but a warning that not following God leads to the same fate as Israel's (aka destruction).

Isaiah 11

Peace on Earth

[1] *A shoot shall come out from the stump of Jesse, and a branch shall grow out of his roots.* [2] *The spirit of the LORD shall rest on him, the spirit of wisdom and understanding, the spirit of counsel and might, the spirit of knowledge and the fear of the LORD.* [3] *His delight shall be in the fear of the LORD. He shall not judge by what his eyes see, or decide by what his ears hear;* [4] *but with righteousness he shall judge the poor, and decide with equity for the meek of the earth; he shall strike the earth with the rod of his mouth, and with the breath of his lips he shall kill the wicked.* [5] *Righteousness shall be the belt around his waist, and faithfulness the belt around his loins.* [6] *The wolf shall live with the lamb, the leopard shall lie down with the kid, the calf and the lion and the fatling together, and a little child shall lead them.* [7] *The cow and the bear shall graze, their young shall lie down together; and the lion shall eat straw like the ox.* [8] *The nursing child shall play over the hole of the asp, and the weaned child shall put its hand on the adder's den.* [9] *They will not hurt or destroy on all my holy mountain; for the earth will be full of the knowledge of the LORD as the waters cover the sea.* [10] *On that day the root of Jesse shall stand as a signal to the peoples; the nations shall inquire of him, and his dwelling shall be glorious.*

Counting Sheep?

Musings

Perhaps one of the most famous passages in Isaiah is this description of the ideal kingdom, headed by a king in the line of David (Jesse being David's father) and ushering in an unprecedented time of peace and prosperity. In Isaiah's time this might have been in reference to the hope for upcoming Hezekiah's kingship of Judah and centuries later used in reference to Jesus. Isaiah's prophecy likes to use the literary style of oracles, which are essentially general idealized predictions about or visions of the future, and this is no exception.

Isaiah 25

Deliverance

6 On this mountain the LORD of hosts will make for all peoples a feast of rich food, a feast of well-aged wines, of rich
food filled with marrow, of well-aged wines strained clear. 7 And he will destroy on this mountain the shroud that is
cast over all peoples, the sheet that is spread over all nations; he will swallow up death forever. 8 Then the Lord GOD
will wipe away the tears from all faces, and the disgrace of his people he will take away from all the earth, for the
LORD has spoken. 9 It will be said on that day, Lo, this is our God; we have waited for him, so that he might save us.
This is the LORD for whom we have waited; let us be glad and rejoice in his salvation.

Feast Your Eyes

Musings

In Isaiah 24 to 27:13 we take a break from the first author of Isaiah (or first Isaiah for short) to later oracles that are thought to have been inserted much later. This vision is more of life after the apocalypse, after the evil have been vanquished and it's time to celebrate. Death is conquered and every need of the righteous remnant is met. This passage is also quoted in 1 Corinthians 15:54 in reference to the resurrection and in Revelation 7:17 in reference to the wiping away of tears at the end times.

Isaiah 35
The Zion King

The wilderness and the dry land shall be glad, the desert shall rejoice and blossom; like the crocus [2] it shall blossom
abundantly, and rejoice with joy and singing. The glory of Lebanon shall be given to it, the majesty of Carmel and
Sharon. They shall see the glory of the LORD, the majesty of our God. [3] Strengthen the weak hands, and make firm
the feeble knees. [4] Say to those who are of a fearful heart, "Be strong, do not fear! Here is your God. He will come with
vengeance, with terrible recompense. He will come and save you." [5] Then the eyes of the blind shall be opened, and
the ears of the deaf unstopped; [6] then the lame shall leap like a deer, and the tongue of the speechless sing for joy. For
waters shall break forth in the wilderness, and streams in the desert; [7] the burning sand shall become a pool, and the
thirsty ground springs of water; the haunt of jackals shall become a swamp, the grass shall become reeds and rushes. [8]
A highway shall be there, and it shall be called the Holy Way; the unclean shall not travel on it, but it shall be for God's
people; no traveler, not even fools, shall go astray. [9] No lion shall be there, nor shall any ravenous beast come up on it;
they shall not be found there, but the redeemed shall walk there. [10] And the ransomed of the LORD shall return, and
come to Zion with singing; everlasting joy shall be upon their heads; they shall obtain joy and gladness, and sorrow
and sighing shall flee away.

A Jackal of All Trades

Musings

Chapters 34-35:10 and 40-55 belong to an anonymous author writing after the time of first Isaiah probably during the Babylonian exile. This oracle envisions the return of a remnant of Israelites returning to Jerusalem. The road leading back through the desert from Babylon is divinely prepared for a safe journey. God is with them and the punishment for prior transgressions is over.

Isaiah 40

Comfort Inn

Comfort, O comfort my people, says your God. [2] Speak tenderly to Jerusalem, and cry to her that she has served her
term, that her penalty is paid, that she has received from the Lord's hand double for all her sins. [3] A voice cries out: "In
the wilderness prepare the way of the LORD, make straight in the desert a highway for our God. [4] Every valley shall
be lifted up, and every mountain and hill be made low; the uneven ground shall become level, and the rough places a
plain. [5] Then the glory of the LORD shall be revealed, and all people shall see it together, for the mouth of the LORD
has spoken." [6] A voice says, "Cry out!" And I said, "What shall I cry?" All people are grass, their constancy is like the
flower of the field. [7] The grass withers, the flower fades, when the breath of the LORD blows upon it; surely the people
are grass. [8] The grass withers, the flower fades; but the word of our God will stand forever. [9] Get you up to a high moun-
tain, O Zion, herald of good tidings; lift up your voice with strength, O Jerusalem, herald of good tidings, lift it up, do
not fear; say to the cities of Judah, "Here is your God!" [10] See, the Lord GOD comes with might, and his arm rules for
him; his reward is with him, and his recompense before him. [11] He will feed his flock like a shepherd; he will gather the
lambs in his arms, and carry them in his bosom, and gently lead the mother sheep.

Under Construction

Musings

Here Isaiah intimates that Israel has been given a double-share of punishment for their sins, so now God is going to make it up to them by removing the obstacles that might prevent rebuilding Jerusalem (Zion). Even the mountains between Babylon and Jerusalem will be leveled to make the road back easy (consistent with the last passage only using more of an interstate highway analogy). God is portrayed as a shepherd lovingly tending the his flock - the restoration will bring God's people to a very close and personal relationship.

Isaiah 42

Gotta Light?

*Here is my servant, whom I uphold, my chosen, in whom my soul delights; I have put my spirit upon him; he will bring
forth justice to the nations. 2 He will not cry or lift up his voice, or make it heard in the street; 3 a bruised reed he will
not break, and a dimly burning wick he will not quench; he will faithfully bring forth justice. 4 He will not grow faint
or be crushed until he has established justice in the earth; and the coastlands wait for his teaching. 5 Thus says God, the
LORD, who created the heavens and stretched them out, who spread out the earth and what comes from it, who gives
breath to the people upon it and spirit to those who walk in it: 6 I am the LORD, I have called you in righteousness, I
have taken you by the hand and kept you; I have given you as a covenant to the people, a light to the nations, 7 to open
the eyes that are blind, to bring out the prisoners from the dungeon, from the prison those who sit in darkness. 8 I am
the LORD, that is my name; my glory I give to no other, nor my praise to idols. 9 See, the former things have come to
pass, and new things I now declare; before they spring forth, I tell you of them.*

Starry Starry Night

Musings

This is one of four so-called servant songs in Isaiah (the others are 49:1-6, 50:4-9, 52:13-53:12) and is steeped in imagery used in Judaism and Christianity alike. For Judaism this proclaims a strong monotheism and suggests that Israel is the shining light to all the nations (a universal example and message). The servant may be Jacob, Moses or the nation of Israel. Second Isaiah's monotheism is the strongest yet in the Old Testament as YHWY is not just the God among gods, but is the only God. Christianity often associates it with Jesus and in Luke 2:32 Simeon even paraphrases this passage in reference to Jesus. Again, the main reference here is that Israel will be the beacon of justice, the example to the nations as result of this second exodus (back to Jerusalem from Babylon).

Isaiah 43

Drinks on the House

*16 Thus says the LORD, who makes a way in the sea, a path in the mighty waters, 17 who brings out chariot and horse,
army and warrior; they lie down, they cannot rise, they are extinguished, quenched like a wick: 18 Do not remem-
ber the former things, or consider the things of old. 19 I am about to do a new thing; now it springs forth, do you not
perceive it? I will make a way in the wilderness and rivers in the desert. 20 The wild animals will honor me, the jack-
als and the ostriches; for I give water in the wilderness, rivers in the desert, to give drink to my chosen people, 21 the
people whom I formed for myself so that they might declare my praise. 22 Yet you did not call upon me, O Jacob; but
you have been weary of me, O Israel! 23 You have not brought me your sheep for burnt offerings, or honored me with
your sacrifices. I have not burdened you with offerings, or wearied you with frankincense. 24 You have not bought me
sweet cane with money, or satisfied me with the fat of your sacrifices. But you have burdened me with your sins; you
have wearied me with your iniquities. 25 I, I am He who blots out your transgressions for my own sake, and I will not
remember your sins.*

The Sermon in the Woods

Musings

More on how the second exodus (Babylon to Jerusalem) will be made easy instead of difficult (per the original exodus from Egypt to Canaan). God also makes the case that God didn't abandon Israel; it was the other way around. They didn't observe temple worship and even when they did, it had not kept them from sin. God suggests the approach that many a coach recommends to their good athletes ... have a short memory when things aren't working (aka keep trying until it's working again). God is looking past the past problems hoping this will set the stage for God's people to do better in the future. Hopefully they will learn from it.

Isaiah 49:1-7

On a Mission from God!

Listen to me, O coastlands, pay attention, you peoples from far away! The LORD called me before I was born, while I was in my mother's womb he named me. [2] He made my mouth like a sharp sword, in the shadow of his hand he hid me; he made me a polished arrow, in his quiver he hid me away. [3] And he said to me, "You are my servant, Israel, in whom I will be glorified." [4] But I said, "I have labored in vain, I have spent my strength for nothing and vanity; yet surely my cause is with the LORD, and my reward with my God." [5] And now the LORD says, who formed me in the womb to be his servant, to bring Jacob back to him, and that Israel might be gathered to him, for I am honored in the sight of the LORD, and my God has become my strength-- [6] he says, "It is too light a thing that you should be my servant to raise up the tribes of Jacob and to restore the survivors of Israel; I will give you as a light to the nations, that my salvation may reach to the end of the earth." [7] Thus says the LORD, the Redeemer of Israel and his Holy One, to one deeply despised, abhorred by the nations, the slave of rulers, "Kings shall see and stand up, princes, and they shall prostrate themselves, because of the LORD, who is faithful, the Holy One of Israel, who has chosen you."

No Womb to Maneuver

Musings

The second servant calling comes from the servant this time, rather than God as before. The servant is named as Israel and is again identified as a light to the nations to save all the earth. In the first servant passage Israel's justice is emphasized, and here it is salvation. Being called in the womb (of Jerusalem aka mom) is a sign that the servant is a prophet. It a way of showing that it is destiny, not a coincidence or an accident, that the prophet fulfills.

Isaiah 49:8-13

Country Roads, Take Me Home

8 Thus says the LORD: In a time of favor I have answered you, on a day of salvation I have helped you; I have kept
you and given you as a covenant to the people, to establish the land, to apportion the desolate heritages; 9 saying to the
prisoners, "Come out," to those who are in darkness, "Show yourselves." They shall feed along the ways, on all the bare
heights shall be their pasture; 10 they shall not hunger or thirst, neither scorching wind nor sun shall strike them down,
for he who has pity on them will lead them, and by springs of water will guide them. 11 And I will turn all my moun-
tains into a road, and my highways shall be raised up. 12 Lo, these shall come from far away, and lo, these from the
north and from the west, and these from the land of Syene. 13 Sing for joy, O heavens, and exult, O earth; break forth,
O mountains, into singing! For the LORD has comforted his people, and will have compassion on his suffering ones.

Rocky Mountain High

Musings

These verses are all about restoration and celebration. The thoughts about re-establishing Jerusalem from the previous verses continue although less about Israel's example and more about the LORD's part in it. It also echoes Isaiah 40 regarding the interstate highway-like ease the LORD will make the return to Jerusalem from Babylon. Other familiar symbolism includes the prisoners are set free, the hungry are fed, light will come to those in darkness and finally the mountains themselves will sing to the glory of it all.

Isaiah 50

Tongue Lashing

[4] The Lord GOD has given me the tongue of a teacher, that I may know how to sustain the weary with a word. Morning by morning he wakens-- wakens my ear to listen as those who are taught. [5] The Lord GOD has opened my ear, and I was not rebellious, I did not turn backward. [6] I gave my back to those who struck me, and my cheeks to those who pulled out the beard; I did not hide my face from insult and spitting. [7] The Lord GOD helps me; therefore I have not been disgraced; therefore I have set my face like flint, and I know that I shall not be put to shame; [8] he who vindicates me is near. Who will contend with me? Let us stand up together. Who are my adversaries? Let them confront me. [9] It is the Lord GOD who helps me; who will declare me guilty? All of them will wear out like a garment; the moth will eat them up.

Cat Got Your Tongue?

Musings

This is part of the third servant song in Isaiah with the servant speaking to the Israelites. In a nutshell, the servant is given God's word to teach to the Israelites, which he does and many reject (to their own peril). No teachers were hurt in the making of this cartoon.

Isaiah 53

Suffering Servant

[7] He was oppressed, and he was afflicted, yet he did not open his mouth; like a lamb that is led to the slaughter, and like
a sheep that before its shearers is silent, so he did not open his mouth. [8] By a perversion of justice he was taken away.
Who could have imagined his future? For he was cut off from the land of the living, stricken for the transgression of
my people. [9] They made his grave with the wicked and his tomb with the rich, although he had done no violence, and
there was no deceit in his mouth. [10] Yet it was the will of the LORD to crush him with pain. When you make his life an
offering for sin, he shall see his offspring, and shall prolong his days; through him the will of the LORD shall prosper.
[11] Out of his anguish he shall see light; he shall find satisfaction through his knowledge. The righteous one, my servant,
shall make many righteous, and he shall bear their iniquities. [12] Therefore I will allot him a portion with the great, and
he shall divide the spoil with the strong; because he poured out himself to death, and was numbered with the transgres-
sors; yet he bore the sin of many, and made intercession for the transgressors.

Silence of the Lambs

Musings

This passage is excerpted from the fourth and last servant song in Isaiah (the full passage is 52:13-53:12). Its original context is most likely in reference to Israel being the servant suffering for the salvation of all of the nations. Isaiah 40 suggested Israel had indeed suffered more than was necessary for just their own transgressions (a double-portion), which might be what was necessary to move from redeemed (or restored) to redeemer (or example) to the other nations. Christianity often uses this passage as a parallel to Jesus as the suffering servant and messiah. Paul also uses it (Isaiah 52:15) in Romans 15:21 as part of the justification for his mission to the Gentiles.

Isaiah 55

Clap Your Hands All You People

10 For as the rain and the snow come down from heaven, and do not return there until they have watered the earth,
making it bring forth and sprout, giving seed to the sower and bread to the eater, 11 so shall my word be that goes out
from my mouth; it shall not return to me empty, but it shall accomplish that which I purpose, and succeed in the thing
for which I sent it. 12 For you shall go out in joy, and be led back in peace; the mountains and the hills before you shall
burst into song, and all the trees of the field shall clap their hands. 13 Instead of the thorn shall come up the cypress;
instead of the brier shall come up the myrtle; and it shall be to the LORD for a memorial, for an everlasting sign that
shall not be cut off.

What is the Sound of One Tree Clapping?

Musings

Chapter 55 ends second Isaiah's oracles with an invitation to abundant life. God's word is compared with water that nurtures all of the earth providing food and everything is coming up roses ... or cypress trees or myrtle. This is a great passage of joy and hope for the future. Trees especially like it.

Isaiah 58

Why People Stare at Prophets

3 "Why do we fast, but you do not see? Why humble ourselves, but you do not notice?" Look, you serve your own interest on your fast day, and oppress all your workers. 4 Look, you fast only to quarrel and to fight and to strike with a wicked fist. Such fasting as you do today will not make your voice heard on high. 5 Is such the fast that I choose, a day to humble oneself? Is it to bow down the head like a bulrush, and to lie in sackcloth and ashes? Will you call this a fast, a day acceptable to the LORD? 6 Is not this the fast that I choose: to loose the bonds of injustice, to undo the thongs of the yoke, to let the oppressed go free, and to break every yoke? 7 Is it not to share your bread with the hungry, and bring the homeless poor into your house; when you see the naked, to cover them, and not to hide yourself from your own kin? 8 Then your light shall break forth like the dawn, and your healing shall spring up quickly; your vindicator shall go before you, the glory of the LORD shall be your rear guard. 9 Then you shall call, and the LORD will answer; you shall cry for help, and he will say, Here I am. If you remove the yoke from among you, the pointing of the finger, the speaking of evil,

The Yoke is On You

Musings

Chapter 56 begins what scholars consider to be third Isaiah, writing just after the return of the Israelites to Jerusalem. The return is not quite all second Isaiah had hoped it would be, rebuilding Jerusalem will be a long hard task, so these oracles are a bit less optimistic and idealistic. This passage is contrasting true and false worship. It's not hard to discern the meaning, God would like sincerity in worship that leads to and results from caring for each other. God is seldom about going through the motions (fasts, sacrifices, rituals) for their own sake, but almost always about living correctly and giving credit where credit is due. Also, beware of eggs in frilly underwear.

Isaiah 60

Rise and Shine!

Arise, shine; for your light has come, and the glory of the LORD has risen upon you. 2 For darkness shall cover the
earth, and thick darkness the peoples; but the LORD will arise upon you, and his glory will appear over you. 3 Nations
shall come to your light, and kings to the brightness of your dawn. 4 Lift up your eyes and look around; they all gather
together, they come to you; your sons shall come from far away, and your daughters shall be carried on their nurses'
arms. 5 Then you shall see and be radiant; your heart shall thrill and rejoice, because the abundance of the sea shall be
brought to you, the wealth of the nations shall come to you. 6 A multitude of camels shall cover you, the young camels
of Midian and Ephah; all those from Sheba shall come. They shall bring gold and frankincense, and shall proclaim the
praise of the LORD.

Religious Camels

Musings

Echoing the optimism of second Isaiah, this oracle is believed to be written shortly after the return to Jerusalem. This is sort of an ode to Jerusalem, looking forward to restoration and a return to prominence among the nations. Camels are pretty happy about their role in this one.

Isaiah 61:1-4

You can Proclaim it, But will they Follow?

The spirit of the Lord GOD is upon me, because the LORD has anointed me; he has sent me to bring good news to the
oppressed, to bind up the brokenhearted, to proclaim liberty to the captives, and release to the prisoners; 2 to proclaim
the year of the Lord's favor, and the day of vengeance of our God; to comfort all who mourn; 3 to provide for those who
mourn in Zion-- to give them a garland instead of ashes, the oil of gladness instead of mourning, the mantle of praise
instead of a faint spirit. They will be called oaks of righteousness, the planting of the LORD, to display his glory. 4 They
shall build up the ancient ruins, they shall raise up the former devastations; they shall repair the ruined cities, the
devastations of many generations.

Isaiah's Gospel - the Prequel

Musings

The prophet is anointed by God, like Elisha, and proclaims the good news of God's restoration of Israel. Many familiar metaphors are used - the captives are freed, mourning turns to joy, Israelites are like plants showing God's glory and Zion (Jerusalem) is restored. Jesus quotes this passage in Luke 4:18-19. Some refer to it in Luke as the Gospel within the Gospel (aka Jesus' mission statement). It is no coincidence that this cartoon will look familiar to those who have read the *Cartoon Gospel of Luke*.

Isaiah 61:10-62:3

Some More Good News!

[10] I will greatly rejoice in the LORD, my whole being shall exult in my God; for he has clothed me with the garments of salvation, he has covered me with the robe of righteousness, as a bridegroom decks himself with a garland, and as a bride adorns herself with her jewels.
[11] For as the earth brings forth its shoots, and as a garden causes what is sown in it to spring up, so the Lord GOD will cause righteousness and praise to spring up before all the nations.
[62:1] For Zion's sake I will not keep silent, and for Jerusalem's sake I will not rest, until her vindication shines out like the dawn, and her salvation like a burning torch.
[2] The nations shall see your vindication, and all the kings your glory; and you shall be called by a new name that the mouth of the LORD will give.
[3] You shall be a crown of beauty in the hand of the LORD, and a royal diadem in the hand of your God.

Salvation is Always in Fashion

Musings

The rest of Chapter 61, and on into 62, eludes again to Israel's place as an example to the nations. Zion (Jerusalem) will be an example of righteousness to all the nations and it will be restored to glory. Fashion divas not withstanding.

Isaiah 62:1-5

For Zion's Sake

For Zion's sake I will not keep silent, and for Jerusalem's sake I will not rest, until her vindication shines out like the
dawn, and her salvation like a burning torch. [2] The nations shall see your vindication, and all the kings your glory; and
you shall be called by a new name that the mouth of the LORD will give. [3] You shall be a crown of beauty in the hand
of the LORD, and a royal diadem in the hand of your God. [4] You shall no more be termed Forsaken, and your land
shall no more be termed Desolate; but you shall be called My Delight Is in Her, and your land Married; for the LORD
delights in you, and your land shall be married. [5] For as a young man marries a young woman, so shall your builder
marry you, and as the bridegroom rejoices over the bride, so shall your God rejoice over you.

Tough Sell

Musings

This passage repeats verses 1-3 but adds 4 and 5. It's a good thing to move up from being called "forsaken" and "desolate" to "My Delight Is in Her" and "Married." Jerusalem's new relationship with God is compared to a marriage, meaning it is closer than ever. Even when prophets get to tell the good news the audience can be tough.

Isaiah 63:7-9

The Presence of the LORD

[7] I will recount the gracious deeds of the LORD, the praiseworthy acts of the LORD, because of all that the LORD has done for us, and the great favor to the house of Israel that he has shown them according to his mercy, according to the abundance of his steadfast love. [8] For he said, "Surely they are my people, children who will not deal falsely"; and he became their savior [9] in all their distress. It was no messenger or angel but his presence that saved them; in his love and in his pity he redeemed them; he lifted them up and carried them all the days of old.

A Housewarming Present for Israel

Musings

The Israelites are reflecting on the mercy and love of God. It is sort of a psalm-like community remembering of what God has done to redeem God's people. Even though this is about God's presence rather than God's presents, is still about God's gifts.

Isaiah 63:16-64:8

You Are the Potter and I am the Clay, O LORD!

16 For you are our father, though Abraham does not know us and Israel does not acknowledge us; you, O LORD, are our
father; our Redeemer from of old is your name. 17 Why, O LORD, do you make us stray from your ways and harden our
heart, so that we do not fear you? Turn back for the sake of your servants, for the sake of the tribes that are your heritage.
18 Your holy people took possession for a little while; but now our adversaries have trampled down your sanctuary. 19 We
have long been like those whom
you do not rule, like those not
called by your name. 64:1 O that
you would tear open the heav-
ens and come down, so that
the mountains would quake at
your presence-- 2 as when fire
kindles brushwood and the fire
causes water to boil-- to make
your name known to your ad-
versaries, so that the nations
might tremble at your presence!
3 When you did awesome deeds
that we did not expect, you came
down, the mountains quaked at
your presence. 4 From ages past
no one has heard, no ear has
perceived, no eye has seen any
God besides you, who works for
those who wait for him. 5 You
meet those who gladly do right,
those who remember you in
your ways. But you were angry,
and we sinned; because you hid
yourself we transgressed. 6 We
have all become like one who is
unclean, and all our righteous
deeds are like a filthy cloth. We
all fade like a leaf, and our iniq-
uities, like the wind, take us away. 7 There is no one who calls on your name, or attempts to take hold of you; for you
have hidden your face from us, and have delivered us into the hand of our iniquity. 8 Yet, O LORD, you are our Father;
we are the clay, and you are our potter; we are all the work of your hand.

Mold Me

Musings

The oracle continues with a frustrated plea from the Israelites. Things are so tough that they argue that Abraham and Israel (Jacob) have abandoned them. They call upon God as father (63.16 and 64:8) (one of the few places that God is referred to as father in the Old Testament) with a direct, yet personal, plea for help. While they seem to be acknowledging their sins, they suggest it is because God hardened their hearts (as God did to Pharaoh) and remained hidden from them (as though they had been trying to find God). This passage ends on a Psalm-like, upbeat, appeal to God as "our Father" and a request for direction - "you are our potter; we are the work of your hand."

Note: Second Isaiah's staunch monotheism is echoed in third Isaiah only in 64:4 (which is possibly paraphrased later by Paul in 1st Corinthians 2:9).

Isaiah 65

And Now for Something Completely Different

17 For I am about to create new heavens and a new earth; the former things shall not be remembered or come to mind.
18 But be glad and rejoice forever in what I am creating; for I am about to create Jerusalem as a joy, and its people as a
delight. 19 I will rejoice in Jerusalem, and delight in my people; no more shall the sound of weeping be heard in it, or the
cry of distress. 20 No more shall there be in it an infant that lives but a few days, or an old person who does not live out
a lifetime; for one who dies at a hundred years will be considered a youth, and one who falls short of a hundred will be
considered accursed. 21 They shall build houses and inhabit them; they shall plant vineyards and eat their fruit. 22 They
shall not build and another inhabit; they shall not plant and another eat; for like the days of a tree shall the days of
my people be, and my chosen shall long enjoy the work of their hands. 23 They shall not labor in vain, or bear children
for calamity; for they shall be offspring blessed by the LORD-- and their descendants as well. 24 Before they call I will
answer, while they are yet speaking I will hear. 25 The wolf and the lamb shall feed together, the lion shall eat straw like
the ox; but the serpent--its food shall be dust! They shall not hurt or destroy on all my holy mountain, says the LORD.

Cheese Tofu-Bugers in Paradise

Musings

This is a picture of the new Jerusalem which will be like the Garden of Eden only better. All will live a full, healthy, happy life (100 or more years), enjoy the fruit of their hands and families. There is joy, peace and harmony in all the land - the wolf, lamb, lion and ox will all eat together and the serpent will be stifled (eat dust). This picture of the new creation is also referred to in the New Testament (2nd Peter 3:13 and Revelation 21) with regard to a post-apocalypse new beginning for the world. You have to admit, it would make for an interesting buffet.

Jeremiah

Jeremiah 1

An Early Womber or a Womb with a View or Womb for Improvement

4 Now the word of the LORD came to me saying, 5 "Before I formed you in the womb I knew you, and before you were
born I consecrated you; I appointed you a prophet to the nations." 6 Then I said, "Ah, Lord GOD! Truly I do not know
how to speak, for I am only a boy." 7 But the LORD said to me, "Do not say, 'I am only a boy'; for you shall go to all
to whom I send you, and you shall speak whatever I command you, 8 Do not be afraid of them, for I am with you to
deliver you, says the LORD." 9 Then the LORD put out his hand and touched my mouth; and the LORD said to me,
"Now I have put my words in your mouth. 10 See, today I appoint you over nations and over kingdoms, to pluck up and
to pull down, to destroy and to overthrow, to build and to plant."

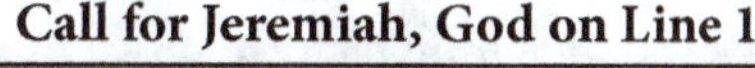

Call for Jeremiah, God on Line 1

Musings

This is Jeremiah's call to be a prophet. It is similar to Moses' calling in that God appoints him, he tries to get out of it, God reassures him that the words he needs will be provided and he finally agrees to it. Unlike Moses though, Jeremiah didn't really have a choice, since he was called in the womb, it was his destiny. Jeremiah isn't just a prophet to Judah but rather to "the nations." To Jeremiah God is at work in all the nations. Even in the calling though, it is clear that Jeremiah is not going to have an easy message - he will be bringing as much bad news as good, but at least the good news comes at the end. Jeremiah is written at about the same times as Isaiah - during the destruction, exile and post-exilic period for the Israelites in Judah.

Jeremiah 3

Sister Act

*7 And I thought, "After she has done all this she will return to me"; but she did not return, and her false sister Judah
saw it. 8 She saw that for all the adulteries of that faithless one, Israel, I had sent her away with a decree of divorce; yet
her false sister Judah did not fear, but she too went and played the whore. 9 Because she took her whoredom so lightly,
she polluted the land, committing adultery with stone and tree. 10 Yet for all this her false sister Judah did not return
to me with her whole heart, but only in pretense, says the LORD. 11 Then the LORD said to me: Faithless Israel has
shown herself less guilty than false Judah. 12 Go, and proclaim these words toward the north, and say: Return, faithless
Israel, says the LORD. I will not look on you in anger, for I am merciful, says the LORD; I will not be angry forever.
13 Only acknowledge your guilt, that you have rebelled against the LORD your God, and scattered your favors among
strangers under every green tree, and have not obeyed my voice, says the LORD. 14 Return, O faithless children, says
the LORD, for I am your master; I will take you, one from a city and two from a family, and I will bring you to Zion.*

Jeremiah Discusses Marketing Strategies with God

Musings

This is a very colorful way of saying that Israel was unfaithful, thus Assyria conquered them, but Judah is even more unfaithful (to God) making their fall inevitable as well. Judah is actually worse because they saw what happened to Israel and didn't learn from it. Jeremiah is sent to Israel to tell them to return to God, since Judah is seemingly not interested in fixing their own situation. God offers to restore Israel if they will repent. Also underlying the message is that it isn't God who abandoned Israel or Judah, but just the opposite. Nothing like a little name calling to get people's attention.

Jeremiah 17

Two in the Shrub are Worth ...

*5 Thus says the LORD: Cursed are those who trust in mere mortals and make mere flesh their strength, whose hearts
turn away from the LORD. 6 They shall be like a shrub in the desert, and shall not see when relief comes. They shall live
in the parched places of the wilderness, in an uninhabited salt land. 7 Blessed are those who trust in the LORD, whose
trust is the LORD. 8 They shall be like a tree planted by water, sending out its roots by the stream. It shall not fear when
heat comes, and its leaves shall stay green; in the year of drought it is not anxious, and it does not cease to bear fruit.
9 The heart is devious above all else; it is perverse-- who can understand it? 10 I the LORD test the mind and search the
heart, to give to all according to their ways, according to the fruit of their doings.*

You Can Run but You Cannot Hide

Musings

This comes after Judah falls and the people are exiled by the Babylonians. It was a result of Judah's corruption and unfaithfulness, yet this poem provides some hope amidst the hardship, basically saying that it is always best to team up with God. Some scholars think it echos Psalm 1 and perhaps later is echoed by Led Zeppelin in their song Stairway to Heaven (Yes there are two paths you can go by, but in the long run, there's still time to change the road you're on). Okay, I doubt Led Zeppelin had this in mind, but it still fits, sort of.

Jeremiah 18

Harry Potter

[1] The word that came to Jeremiah from the LORD: [2] "Come, go down to the potter's house, and there I will let you hear my words." [3] So I went down to the potter's house, and there he was working at his wheel. [4] The vessel he was making of clay was spoiled in the potter's hand, and he reworked it into another vessel, as seemed good to him. [5] Then the word of the LORD came to me: [6] Can I not do with you, O house of Israel, just as this potter has done? says the LORD. Just like the clay in the potter's hand, so are you in my hand, O house of Israel. [7] At one moment I may declare concerning a nation or a kingdom, that I will pluck up and break down and destroy it, [8] but if that nation, concerning which I have spoken, turns from its evil, I will change my mind about the disaster that I intended to bring on it. [9] And at another moment I may declare concerning a nation or a kingdom that I will build and plant it, [10] but if it does evil in my sight, not listening to my voice, then I will change my mind about the good that I had intended to do to it. [11] Now, therefore, say to the people of Judah and the inhabitants of Jerusalem: Thus says the LORD: Look, I am a potter shaping evil against you and devising a plan against you. Turn now, all of you from your evil way, and amend your ways and your doings.

Getting Clay Feet

Musings

This might also be titled "Have I Got a Deal for You." The parable or analogy is clear, God is like a potter who can even take the mess Judah has become and make it into something useful. God is shown again here as being in control of all events, so that if things are not working out, God can use whatever means God desires to fix them. So God is making an offer that Judah should not refuse, but in verse 12 (not included above) that's exactly what they do (refuse) thus sealing their own fate. Even though God is in control, they had a choice.

Jeremiah 20

Pashhur-ized

1 Now the priest Pashhur son of Immer, who was chief officer in the house of the LORD, heard Jeremiah prophesying these
things. 2 Then Pashhur struck the prophet Jeremiah, and put him in the stocks that were in the upper Benjamin Gate of the
house of the LORD. 3 The next morning when Pashhur released Jeremiah from the stocks, Jeremiah said to him, The LORD
has named you not Pashhur but "Terror-all-around." 4 For thus says the LORD: I am making you a terror to yourself and
to all your friends; and they shall fall by the sword of their enemies while you look on. And I will give all Judah into the
hand of the king of Babylon; he shall carry
them captive to Babylon, and shall kill them
with the sword. 5 I will give all the wealth of
this city, all its gains, all its prized belong-
ings, and all the treasures of the kings of Ju-
dah into the hand of their enemies, who shall
plunder them, and seize them, and carry
them to Babylon. 6 And you, Pashhur, and all
who live in your house, shall go into captivity,
and to Babylon you shall go; there you shall
die, and there you shall be buried, you and
all your friends, to whom you have proph-
esied falsely. 7 O LORD, you have enticed me,
and I was enticed; you have overpowered
me, and you have prevailed. I have become
a laughingstock all day long; everyone mocks
me. 8 For whenever I speak, I must cry out, I
must shout, "Violence and destruction!" For
the word of the LORD has become for me a
reproach and derision all day long. 9 If I say,
"I will not mention him, or speak any more
in his name," then within me there is some-
thing like a burning fire shut up in my bones;
I am weary with holding it in, and I cannot.
10 For I hear many whispering: "Terror is all
around! Denounce him! Let us denounce
him!" All my close friends are watching for
me to stumble. "Perhaps he can be enticed,
and we can prevail against him, and take our
revenge on him." 11 But the LORD is with me
like a dread warrior; therefore my persecu-
tors will stumble, and they will not prevail.
They will be greatly shamed, for they will not
succeed. Their eternal dishonor will never be
forgotten. 12 O LORD of hosts, you test the
righteous, you see the heart and the mind; let me see your retribution upon them, for to you I have committed my cause. 13
Sing to the LORD; praise the LORD! For he has delivered the life of the needy from the hands of evildoers.

If I've Told You Once ...

Musings

Well it sucks to be the high priest Passhhur. He doesn't believe Jeremiah's prophecy and tries to suppress his message. As a result he gets a new name "terror all around" and the future isn't looking too good for him and his friends and family. Jeremiah points out poetically (from verse 7 on) that he doesn't want to be the bearer of bad news, but he has no choice. God picked him and compels him to deliver the message he is given.

Jeremiah 23

Sleep on This

1 Woe to the shepherds who destroy and scatter the sheep of my pasture! says the LORD. 2 Therefore thus says the
LORD, the God of Israel, concerning the shepherds who shepherd my people: It is you who have scattered my flock,
and have driven them away, and you have not attended to them. So I will attend to you for your evil doings, says the
LORD. 3 Then I myself will gather the remnant of my flock out of all the lands where I have driven them, and I will
bring them back to their fold, and they shall be fruitful and multiply. 4 I will raise up shepherds over them who will
shepherd them, and they shall not fear any longer, or be dismayed, nor shall any be missing, says the LORD. 5 The days
are surely coming, says the LORD, when I will raise up for David a righteous Branch, and he shall reign as king and
deal wisely, and shall execute justice and righteousness in the land. 6 In his days Judah will be saved and Israel will live
in safety. And this is the name by which he will be called: "The LORD is our righteousness."

Accounting Sheep

Musings

Judah's corrupt leadership is the cause of its fall, but in due time God will save a remnant, give them a good davidic king and all will be well with Judah and Israel once again. The restored kingdoms are seen as a return to one kingdom and under one king in the davidic line, perhaps harkening back to a time before Israel split from Judah and they were at their strongest (under Saul, David and finally Solomon). Apparently sheep are way more talented that generally given credit (or debit) for.

Jeremiah 28

Yoking Around with the King

*1 In that same year, at the beginning of the reign of King Zedekiah of Judah, in the fifth month of the fourth year, the prophet
Hananiah son of Azzur, from Gibeon, spoke to me in the house of the LORD, in the presence of the priests and all the people,
saying, 2 "Thus says the LORD of hosts, the God of Israel: I have broken the yoke of the king of Babylon. 3 Within two years
I will bring back to this place all the vessels of the Lord's house, which King Nebuchadnezzar of Babylon took away from
this place and carried to Babylon. 4 I will also bring back to this place King Jeconiah son of Jehoiakim of Judah, and all the
exiles from Judah who went to Babylon, says the LORD, for I will break the yoke of the king of Babylon." 5 Then the prophet
Jeremiah spoke to the prophet Hananiah in the presence of the priests and all the people who were standing in the house of
the LORD; 6 and the prophet Jeremiah said, "Amen! May the LORD do so; may the LORD fulfill the words that you have
prophesied, and bring back to this place from Babylon the vessels of the house of the LORD, and all the exiles. 7 But listen
now to this word that I speak in your hearing and in the hearing of all the people. 8 The prophets who preceded you and me
from ancient times prophesied war, famine, and pestilence against many countries and great kingdoms. 9 As for the prophet
who prophesies peace, when the word of that prophet comes true, then it will be known that the LORD has truly sent the
prophet."*

Yolk's On You

Musings

Jeremiah wishes his competing prophet, Hananiah, well but suggests there may be some doubt. Indeed that proves to be the case. Even though Nebuchadnezzar eventually loses power, it's not going to be when Hananiah predicts and worse for Hananiah, Jeremiah goes on to discredit him (vs. 10-17) and he dies later that year. It's not really clear why this was selected as a lectionary passage in that the verses selected tell a partial story of little consequence, but it does lend validity to Jeremiah as a prophet and shed some light on false prophecy (and bad eggs).

Jeremiah 31:1-6

Everlasting Love

At that time, says the LORD, I will be the God of all the families of Israel, and they shall be my people. [2] *Thus says the*
LORD: The people who survived the sword found grace in the wilderness; when Israel sought for rest, [3] *the LORD ap-*
peared to him from far away. I have loved you with an everlasting love; therefore I have continued my faithfulness to
you. [4] *Again I will build you, and you shall be built, O virgin Israel! Again you shall take your tambourines, and go*
forth in the dance of the merrymakers. [5] *Again you shall plant vineyards on the mountains of Samaria; the planters*
shall plant, and shall enjoy the fruit. [6] *For there shall be a day when sentinels will call in the hill country of Ephraim:*
"Come, let us go up to Zion, to the LORD our God."

Amazing Grace

Musings

This is a very upbeat view of the return from exile. Israel will be restored to one nation, prior to the split between Northern (Israel) and Southern (Judah) kingdoms. God will forget their adulterous past, hence the term virgin Israel, and continue God's faithfulness to them. Samaria and Ephraim are names for the Northern Kingdom and their agriculture will flourish and all the people will go to Zion (Jerusalem). All-in-all the return is to be a glorious time of celebration and re-unification. Grace will be found, whether she wants to be or not.

Jeremiah 31:7-14

Have a Nice Day

*7 For thus says the LORD: Sing aloud with gladness for Jacob, and raise shouts for the chief of the nations; proclaim,
give praise, and say, "Save, O LORD, your people, the remnant of Israel." 8 See, I am going to bring them from the land
of the north, and gather them from the farthest parts of the earth, among them the blind and the lame, those with child
and those in labor, together; a great company, they shall return here. 9 With weeping they shall come, and with consola-
tions I will lead them back, I will let them walk by brooks of water, in a straight path in which they shall not stumble;
for I have become a father to Israel, and Ephraim is my firstborn. 10 Hear the word of the LORD, O nations, and declare
it in the coastlands far away; say, "He who scattered Israel will gather him, and will keep him as a shepherd a flock." 11
For the LORD has ransomed Jacob, and has redeemed him from hands too strong for him. 12 They shall come and sing
aloud on the height of Zion, and they shall be radiant over the goodness of the LORD, over the grain, the wine, and
the oil, and over the young of the flock and the herd; their life shall become like a watered garden, and they shall never
languish again. 13 Then shall the young women rejoice in the dance, and the young men and the old shall be merry. I
will turn their mourning into joy, I will comfort them, and give them gladness for sorrow. 14 I will give the priests their
fill of fatness, and my people shall be satisfied with my bounty, says the LORD.*

Happy Days are Here Again

Musings

This is a vision or oracle similar to several in Isaiah (25, 40, 49, 55) and earlier in Jeremiah 23 of the restoration of Israel. What God scattered will now be brought back together and made even better. It will be a joyous time and all will live long and be satisfied. I'm guessing Jeremiah much prefers these messages to the others he's had to deliver.

Jeremiah 31:31-34

Learning the Law by Heart

*[31] The days are surely coming, says the LORD, when I will make a new covenant with the house of Israel and the house
of Judah. [32] It will not be like the covenant that I made with their ancestors when I took them by the hand to bring
them out of the land of Egypt--a covenant that they broke, though I was their husband, says the LORD. [33] But this is
the covenant that I will make with the house of Israel after those days, says the LORD: I will put my law within them,
and I will write it on their hearts; and I will be their God, and they shall be my people. [34] No longer shall they teach
one another, or say to each other, "Know the LORD," for they shall all know me, from the least of them to the greatest,
says the LORD; for I will forgive their iniquity, and remember their sin no more.*

Two Tablets for Your Heart

Musings

Continuing with the thoughts on how great it's going to be, God will make a new covenant. This covenant will be better than the one made on Mount Sinai, which the people broke. God will restore the direct relationship with the people and this time write the law on their hearts. This refers most directly to the return to and rebuilding of Jerusalem by the Israelite remnant after the Babylonian exile. Later it is referenced by Christianity in regard to Jesus' mission and echoed in Paul's letters when he suggests that the law has been superseded.

Jeremiah 33

Methaphors of a Cyrptic God

[14] The days are surely coming, says the LORD, when I will fulfill the promise I made to the house of Israel and the house of Judah. [15] In those days and at that time I will cause a righteous Branch to spring up for David; and he shall execute justice and righteousness in the land. [16] In those days Judah will be saved and Jerusalem will live in safety. And this is the name by which it will be called: "The LORD is our righteousness."

Tales from the Crypt

Musings

Jeremiah Chapters 30-33 is dubbed "the little book of consolation." It ends here with a final vision of the davidic kingdom returning to Judah and Israel (also mentioned elsewhere such as chapter 23) to prominence. Significant for the Israelites because it harkens back to their greatest kingdoms (David's and his son Solomon's) and significant in Christianity due to Jesus' davidic link. However, other than a brief independence under the Maccabees (the Hasmonean dynasty) Israel was not an autonomous nation since Judah's final fall to the Babylonians and until the modern nation was formed in 1948 after World War II.

Ezekiel
Ezekiel 18
Sour Grapes

1 The word of the LORD came to me: 2 What do you mean by repeating this proverb concerning the land of Israel, "The
parents have eaten sour grapes, and the children's teeth are set on edge"? 3 As I live, says the Lord GOD, this proverb
shall no more be used by you in Israel. 4 Know that all lives are mine; the life of the parent as well as the life of the child is
mine: it is only the person who sins that shall die. 5 If a man is righteous and does what is lawful and right-- 6 if he does
not eat upon the mountains or lift up his eyes to the idols of the house of Israel, does not defile his neighbor's wife or ap-
proach a woman during her menstrual period, 7 does not oppress anyone, but restores to the debtor his pledge, commits
no robbery, gives his bread to the hungry and covers the naked with a garment, 8 does not take advance or accrued in-
terest, withholds his hand from iniquity, executes true justice between contending parties, 9 follows my statutes, and is
careful to observe my ordinances, acting faithfully--such a one is righteous; he shall surely live, says the Lord GOD. .... 24 But
when the righteous turn away from their righteousness and commit iniquity and do the same abominable things that the wicked do, shall they live? None of the righteous deeds that they have done shall be remembered; for the treachery of which they are guilty and the sin they have committed, they shall die. 25 Yet
you say, "The way of the Lord is unfair." Hear now, O house of Israel: Is my way unfair? Is it not your ways that are unfair? 26
When the righteous turn away from their righteousness and commit iniquity, they shall die for it; for the iniquity that they have committed they shall die.
27 Again, when the wicked turn away from the wickedness they have committed and do what is lawful and right, they shall save their life. 28 Because they consid-
ered and turned away from all the transgressions that they had committed, they shall surely live; they shall not die. 29 Yet the house of Israel says, "The
way of the Lord is unfair." O house of Israel, are my ways unfair? Is it not your ways that are unfair?

Outrageous Demands

Musings

Ezekiel attempts to answer the question of how God could allow Judah to be defeated, the temple destroyed, and the people dispersed. He quotes a proverb representing a fatalistic view of God's sovereignty and then explains why this is not true. They can return to God's favor by essentially living by the law. In a sense, it's the grace side of the 2nd Commandment (Exodus 20:5-6) showing favor to those who follow God's commandments. He counters their arguments that God is unfair by suggesting that God's righteousness is fair, but it is their ways that are not.

Ezekiel 33

Sound the Alarm

1 The word of the LORD came to me: 2 O Mortal, speak to your people and say to them, If I bring the sword upon a land,
and the people of the land take one of their number as their sentinel; 3 and if the sentinel sees the sword coming upon the
land and blows the trumpet and warns the people; 4 then if any who hear the sound of the trumpet do not take warn-
ing, and the sword comes and takes them away, their blood shall be upon their own heads. 5 They heard the sound of
the trumpet and did not take warning; their blood shall be upon themselves. But if they had taken warning, they would
have saved their lives. 6 But if the sentinel sees the sword coming and does not blow the trumpet, so that the people are not
warned, and the sword comes
and takes any of them, they are
taken away in their iniquity, but
their blood I will require at the
sentinel's hand. 7 So you, mortal,
I have made a sentinel for the
house of Israel; whenever you
hear a word from my mouth,
you shall give them warning
from me. 8 If I say to the wicked,
"O wicked ones, you shall surely
die," and you do not speak to
warn the wicked to turn from
their ways, the wicked shall die
in their iniquity, but their blood
I will require at your hand. 9
But if you warn the wicked to
turn from their ways, and they
do not turn from their ways,
the wicked shall die in their in-
iquity, but you will have saved
your life. 10 Now you, mortal,
say to the house of Israel, Thus
you have said: "Our transgres-
sions and our sins weigh upon
us, and we waste away because
of them; how then can we live?"
11 Say to them, As I live, says the
Lord GOD, I have no pleasure
in the death of the wicked, but that the wicked turn from their ways and live; turn back, turn back from your evil ways;
for why will you die, O house of Israel?

The Boogie-Woogie Bugle Boy of Company B

Musings

This opens with an explanation of the wartime responsibilities of the people and their sentinel and it ends with the focus on the role of the sentinel, which is Ezekiel. It echoes the plea of Chapter 18 to turn from evil ways, explaining that God wants them to be spared. While this is an indictment of Judah for abandoning God, it leaves hope to turn it around. In a few verses (21-22) it is clear that Jerusalem has fallen, yet Chapters 33-39 begin to change the tone from destruction toward restoration. So while they have lost their home, Ezekiel is telling them not to lose all hope. Let's hope no vuvuzelas were involved.

Ezekiel 34

The Good Shepherd

11 For thus says the Lord GOD: I myself will search for my sheep, and will seek them out. 12 As shepherds seek out their flocks when they are among their scattered sheep, so I will seek out my sheep. I will rescue them from all the places to which they have been scattered on a day of clouds and thick darkness. 13 I will bring them out from the peoples and gather them from the countries, and will bring them into their own land; and I will feed them on the mountains of Israel, by the watercourses, and in all the inhabited parts of the land. 14 I will feed them with good pasture, and the mountain heights of Israel shall be their pasture; there they shall lie down in good grazing land, and they shall feed on rich pasture on the mountains of Israel. 15 I myself will be the shepherd of my sheep, and I will make them lie down, says the Lord GOD. 16 I will seek the lost, and I will bring back the strayed, and I will bind up the injured, and I will strengthen the weak, but the fat and the strong I will destroy. I will feed them with justice.

Culling the Herd

Musings

Ezekiel proclaims God as the one true shepherd who will seek out God's sheep, restore the weak, find the lost, heal the injured and provide them rest. I'm guessing that the fat and strong sheep are those that did evil to the others either directly or indirectly, or continued to disobey God. Other places that mention the Lord as shepherd include Psalm 23, Isaiah 40:11, and John 10:1-18. Sheep generally get good PR in the Bible.

Ezekiel 37

Dry Bones

1 The hand of the LORD came upon me, and he brought me out by the spirit of the LORD and set me down in the middle
of a valley; it was full of bones. 2 He led me all around them; there were very many lying in the valley, and they were very
dry. 3 He said to me, "Mortal, can these bones live?" I answered, "O Lord GOD, you know." 4 Then he said to me, "Proph-
esy to these bones, and say to them: O dry bones, hear the word of the LORD. 5 Thus says the Lord GOD to these bones:
I will cause breath to enter you, and you shall live. 6 I will lay sinews on you, and will cause flesh to come upon you, and
cover you with skin, and put breath in you, and you shall live; and you shall know that I am the LORD." 7 So I prophe-
sied as I had been commanded; and as I prophesied, suddenly there was a noise, a rattling, and the bones came togeth-
er, bone to its bone. 8 I looked,
and there were sinews on them,
and flesh had come upon them,
and skin had covered them; but
there was no breath in them. 9
Then he said to me, "Prophesy
to the breath, prophesy, mor-
tal, and say to the breath: Thus
says the Lord GOD: Come from
the four winds, O breath, and
breathe upon these slain, that
they may live." 10 I prophesied
as he commanded me, and the
breath came into them, and
they lived, and stood on their
feet, a vast multitude. 11 Then he
said to me, "Mortal, these bones
are the whole house of Israel.
They say, 'Our bones are dried
up, and our hope is lost; we
are cut off completely.' 12 There-
fore prophesy, and say to them,
Thus says the Lord GOD: I am
going to open your graves, and
bring you up from your graves,
O my people; and I will bring
you back to the land of Israel.
13 And you shall know that I am
the LORD, when I open your
graves, and bring you up from your graves, O my people. 14 I will put my spirit within you, and you shall live, and I will
place you on your own soil; then you shall know that I, the LORD, have spoken and will act," says the LORD.

Sports Drink Proving Grounds

Musings

Probably one of the more well-known stories in the Old Testament is Ezekiel and the dry bones. It answers the question as to whether God can bring back to life a "dead" people (a.k.a. Israel). The answer is "Yes" of course. I would not be surprised if Ezekiel didn't often feel like he was prophesying to a bunch of corpses, so this experiment (real or metaphorical) probably serves to boost his spirits as well as the Israelites. Modern day sports drink manufacturers - eat your heart out!

Daniel
Daniel 7
Check the Coffee

9 As I watched, thrones were set in place, and an Ancient One took his throne, his clothing was white as snow, and the
hair of his head like pure wool; his throne was fiery flames, and its wheels were burning fire. 10 A stream of fire issued and
flowed out from his presence.
A thousand thousands served
him, and ten thousand times
ten thousand stood attending
him. The court sat in judgment,
and the books were opened. 11
I watched then because of the
noise of the arrogant words that
the horn was speaking. And as
I watched, the beast was put to
death, and its body destroyed
and given over to be burned
with fire. 12 As for the rest of
the beasts, their dominion was
taken away, but their lives were
prolonged for a season and
a time. 13 As I watched in the
night visions, I saw one like a
human being coming with the
clouds of heaven. And he came
to the Ancient One and was
presented before him. 14 To him
was given dominion and glory
and kingship, that all peoples,
nations, and languages should
serve him. His dominion is an
everlasting dominion that shall
not pass away, and his kingship
is one that shall never be de-
stroyed.

Sheepish

Musings

The first half of Daniel concerns the stories about Daniel and friends, and the second half records four apocalyptic visions attributed to Daniel. This excerpt is part of the first vision. In verses 1-8 (just prior to this excerpt) four beasts are described representing Babylon (lion), the Medes (bear), the Persians (leopard) and the Greeks (dragon). In these verses (9-14) the ancient one, God, is seated on the fiery throne and destroys the Greeks (the horn is Antiochus IV Epiphanes). The other nations aren't destroyed just yet. Kingship is given to "one like a human." This is another way of saying the "Son of Man" or Messiah. The Son of Man here has been interpreted in different ways including as symbolic of the faithful Jew or as an angelic being like Michael. Of course the imagery here is found in other books of the Bible including Job, Isaiah, and Revelation. In Revelation and the Gospels the Son of Man is used in reference to Jesus, thus bridging Old Testament prophecies to the New Testament. A sheep on the thrown might be a bit of a stretch, but like I said before, they have good PR.

Hosea

Hosea 2

Fatal Attraction

14 Therefore, I will now allure her, and bring her into the wilderness, and speak tenderly to her. 15 From there I will give
her her vineyards, and make the Valley of Achor a door of hope. There she shall respond as in the days of her youth,
as at the time when she came out of the land of Egypt. 16 On that day, says the LORD, you will call me, "My husband,"
and no longer will you call me, "My Baal." 17 For I will remove the names of the Baals from her mouth, and they shall
be mentioned by name no more. 18 I will make for you a covenant on that day with the wild animals, the birds of the
air, and the creeping things of the ground; and I will abolish the bow, the sword, and war from the land; and I will
make you lie down in safety. 19 And I will take you for my wife forever; I will take you for my wife in righteousness and
in justice, in steadfast love, and in mercy. 20 I will take you for my wife in faithfulness; and you shall know the LORD.

Israel at the Dentist

Musings

Hosea is a very interesting prophet with a very unusual way conveying his message. He is called by God to be a prophet, to marry a harlot and to the name his kids with symbolic names (such as Lo Ruhamah "no mercy" and Lo Ammi "not my people"). The idea of Israel acting the harlot wasn't new (Jeremiah 3 for example), but actually living it out was. (The kids probably weren't too happy about it either.) That aside, this passage is calling Israel back into faithfulness to God - if they comply their relationships will be restored. God stands as the wronged husband willing to forgive and take back his unfaithful wife (Israel) and children (the Israelites) and make things better than they were before. It will lead to a "happily ever after" ending. Politically Hosea is suggesting Israel allying with Assyria is bad (part of why they are unfaithful) and Aram (Syria) is good.

Hosea 4

Missing the Point

[1] Hear the word of the LORD, O people of Israel; for the LORD has an indictment against the inhabitants of the land. There is no faithfulness or loyalty, and no knowledge of God in the land. [2] Swearing, lying, and murder, and stealing and adultery break out; bloodshed follows bloodshed. [3] Therefore the land mourns, and all who live in it languish; together with the wild animals and the birds of the air, even the fish of the sea are perishing. [...] [5:15] I will return again to my place until they acknowledge their guilt and seek my face. In their distress they will beg my favor: [6:1] "Come, let us return to the LORD; for it is he who has torn, and he will heal us; he has struck down, and he will bind us up. [2] After two days he will revive us; on the third day he will raise us up, that we may live before him. [3] Let us know, let us press on to know the LORD; his appearing is as sure as the dawn; he will come to us like the showers, like the spring rains that water the earth." [4] What shall I do with you, O Ephraim? What shall I do with you, O Judah? Your love is like a morning cloud, like the dew that goes away early. [5] Therefore I have hewn them by the prophets, I have killed them by the words of my mouth, and my judgment goes forth as the light. [6] For I desire steadfast love and not sacrifice, the knowledge of God rather than burnt offerings.

Chew on This

Musings

God makes a case against Israel for breaking the covenant. Israel is violating most of the ten commandments; they aren't faithful to God; nor do they seem to have any relationship (or knowledge) of God. Everything suffers as a result since the covenant includes all creation. Therefore, in Verse 5:15, God abandons Israel. Hosea then calls for Israel to repent. The three-day restoration cycle probably reinterprets a Canaanite fertility mythology showing that it is God who is in control of the rain and who can bring them true help. Finally the excerpts end with sort of a lament that neither Israel or Judah heed their prophets (or God) and what God really wants is their hearts, not their rituals.

Hosea 11

What Am I - Chopped Liver?

1 When Israel was a child, I loved him, and out of Egypt I called my son. 2 The more I called them, the more they went
from me; they kept sacrificing to the Baals, and offering incense to idols. 3 Yet it was I who taught Ephraim to walk, I
took them up in my arms; but
they did not know that I healed
them. 4 I led them with cords of
human kindness, with bands of
love. I was to them like those
who lift infants to their cheeks.
I bent down to them and fed
them. 5 They shall return to
the land of Egypt, and Assyria
shall be their king, because they
have refused to return to me.
6 The sword rages in their cit-
ies, it consumes their oracle-
priests, and devours because
of their schemes. 7 My people
are bent on turning away from
me. To the Most High they call,
but he does not raise them up
at all. 8 How can I give you
up, Ephraim? How can I hand
you over, O Israel? How can I
make you like Admah? How
can I treat you like Zeboiim?
My heart recoils within me; my
compassion grows warm and
tender. 9 I will not execute my
fierce anger; I will not again
destroy Ephraim; for I am God
and no mortal, the Holy One in
your midst, and I will not come in wrath. 10 They shall go after the LORD, who roars like a lion; when he roars, his
children shall come trembling from the west. 11 They shall come trembling like birds from Egypt, and like doves from
the land of Assyria; and I will return them to their homes, says the LORD.

You Never Call

Musings

Basically Israel (and Judah) are acting like ungrateful brats, yet God loves them anyway. God was with them in Egypt, during the Exodus, as they formed a nation, and yet now they show no faith or gratitude and, perhaps worse, "*are bent on turning away from me.*" God will allow (or appoint) Egypt and Assyria to rule over them. Even so instead of God's wrath, which they deserve, they will get God's love and compassion. C.S. Lewis had to love this passage.

Note: Admah and Zeboiim were cities that got destroyed along with Sodom and Gamorrah.

Joel

Joel 2

I Have a Dream

23 O children of Zion, be glad and rejoice in the LORD your God; for he has given the early rain for your vindication,
he has poured down for you abundant rain, the early and the later rain, as before. 24 The threshing floors shall be full of
grain, the vats shall overflow with wine and oil. 25 I will repay you for the years that the swarming locust has eaten, the
hopper, the destroyer, and the cutter, my great army, which I sent against you. 26 You shall eat in plenty and be satisfied,
and praise the name of the LORD your God, who has dealt wondrously with you. And my people shall never again be
put to shame. 27 You shall know that I am in the midst of Israel, and that I, the LORD, am your God and there is no
other. And my people shall never again be put to shame. 28 Then afterward I will pour out my spirit on all flesh; your
sons and your daughters shall prophesy, your old men shall dream dreams, and your young men shall see visions. 29
Even on the male and female slaves, in those days, I will pour out my spirit. 30 I will show portents in the heavens and
on the earth, blood and fire and columns of smoke.

When It Rains, It Pours

Musings

Joel is a prophet most likely in the 5th century BCE, probably in the early Hellenistic period (Greek rule) and Israel and Judah united again (under Greek control). There has just been a locust devastation that Joel views is punishment from God. The people repent and this passage picks up with God's response and promise for the future. Things are going to be very good and there will be a time of plenty and peace. Perhaps the most famous quote from Joel is verse 29 where the relationship with God will be so intimate that prophesy, dreams and visions of God's goodness will be widespread. Umbrella sales will be up.

Amos

Amos 5:6-15

Hate Evil and Love Good

6 Seek the LORD and live, or he will break out against the house of Joseph like fire, and it will devour Bethel, with no
one to quench it. 7 Ah, you that turn justice to wormwood, and bring righteousness to the ground! [...] 10 They hate
the one who reproves in the gate, and they abhor the one who speaks the truth. 11 Therefore because you trample on
the poor and take from them levies of grain, you have built houses of hewn stone, but you shall not live in them; you
have planted pleasant vineyards, but you shall not drink their wine. 12 For I know how many are your transgressions,
and how great are your sins-- you who afflict the righteous, who take a bribe, and push aside the needy in the gate. 13
Therefore the prudent will keep silent in such a time; for it is an evil time. 14 Seek good and not evil, that you may live;
and so the LORD, the God of hosts, will be with you, just as you have said. 15 Hate evil and love good, and establish
justice in the gate; it may be that the LORD, the God of hosts, will be gracious to the remnant of Joseph.

Get With the Program

Musings

Amos is a prophet to Israel (the Northern kingdom) in the time prior to the Assyrian takeover and his main concern seems to be internal social justice. The book is a loose collection of oracles with no particular order or flow to it. In this passage Amos is clearly calling Israel to social justice. Hopefully by protecting the weak and helping the downtrodden (and not taking advantage of them) that will keep them in God's favor. Even worms get their day.

Amos 5:18-24

Lions and Bears and Snakes, Oh My!

18 Alas for you who desire the day of the LORD! Why do you want the day of the LORD? It is darkness, not light; 19 as
if someone fled from a lion, and was met by a bear; or went into the house and rested a hand against the wall, and
was bitten by a snake. 20 Is not the day of the LORD darkness, not light, and gloom with no brightness in it? 21 I hate, I
despise your festivals, and I take no delight in your solemn assemblies. 22 Even though you offer me your burnt offerings
and grain offerings, I will not accept them; and the offerings of well-being of your fatted animals I will not look upon.
23 Take away from me the noise of your songs; I will not listen to the melody of your harps. 24 But let justice roll down
like waters, and righteousness like an ever-flowing stream.

Really Fast Food!

Musings

Amos' optimism turns to warning as he suggests that the expected "day of the LORD" could turn ugly rather than be the good thing that is expected. Rather than be a day of triumph for Israel it could be the day of their destruction. All the cultic worship they can muster won't save them if it is insincere. So he should have had their undivided attention by the time he got to "*But let justice roll down like waters, and righteousness like an ever-flowing stream.*" Perhaps one of the most well-known verses of Amos. While not good for sacrificing, it might be good practice for carrying the Olympic torch.

Jonah

Jonah 3

Mask, Fins and Salvation

1 The word of the LORD came to Jonah a second time, saying, 2 "Get up, go to Nineveh, that great city, and proclaim
to it the message that I tell you." 3 So Jonah set out and went to Nineveh, according to the word of the LORD. Now
Nineveh was an exceedingly large city, a three days' walk across. 4 Jonah began to go into the city, going a day's walk.
And he cried out, "Forty days more, and Nineveh shall be overthrown!" 5 And the people of Nineveh believed God; they
proclaimed a fast, and everyone, great and small, put on sackcloth.

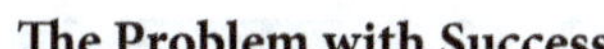

The Problem with Success

Musings

Jonah is tasked with going and telling his enemies that they are going to get destroyed by God. Even though he really didn't want to go (the whole swallowed by a fish thing), he did finally show up and deliver the message. The only problem is that Nineveh chose to believe him and repented and is spared. A few lessons seem to pop right out of this story. First, Jonah is taught through a calamity of his errors that God can show mercy to whom God chooses (so get over it and himself). Second, Nineveh's greatly exaggerated repentance to the warnings from a God they don't know or worship is in ironic contrast to Israel's own response (or lack thereof). The four short chapters of Jonah are well worth reading, especially with the help of a good commentary. It is fun and full of wit and allegory. It clearly illustrates that God is a God of grace and compassion as well as humor. Perhaps the only precursor to snorkeling in the Bible.

Micah
Micah 1
Guess Who's Ticked!?

[2] Hear, you peoples, all of you; listen, O earth, and all that is in it; and let the Lord GOD be a witness against you, the
Lord from his holy temple. [...] [2:1] Alas for those who devise wickedness and evil deeds on their beds! When the morn-
ing dawns, they perform it, because it is in their power. [2] They covet fields, and seize them; houses, and take them away;
they oppress householder and house, people and their inheritance. [3] Therefore thus says the LORD: Now, I am devising
against this family an evil from which you cannot remove your necks; and you shall not walk haughtily, for it will be an evil
time. [4] On that day they shall take up a taunt song against you, and wail with bitter lamentation, and say, "We are utterly ruined; the LORD alters the inheritance of my people; how he removes it from me! Among our captors he parcels
out our fields." [5] Therefore you will have no one to cast the line by lot in the assembly of the
LORD. [6] "Do not preach"--thus they preach-- "one should not preach of such things; disgrace
will not overtake us." [7] Should this be said, O house of Jacob? Is the Lord's patience exhausted? Are these his doings? Do not my words do good to one who
walks uprightly? [8] But you rise up against my people as an enemy; you strip the robe from the peaceful, from those who pass by trustingly with no thought of
war. [9] The women of my people

The Bad News Is ...

you drive out from their pleasant houses; from their young children you take away my glory forever. [10] Arise and go;
for this is no place to rest, because of uncleanness that destroys with a grievous destruction.

Musings

Micah's oracles were intended mostly for Jerusalem (the Southern kingdom of Judah) probably before and just after the fall of Israel (the Northern kingdom) to the Assyrians. Micah often refers to Judah in broader terms as Israel (or Jacob) and is more concerned about the mosaic covenant with God than the davidic one. This passage is about as straight-forward as it gets - Micah is telling Jerusalem in no uncertain terms that it is socially corrupt and God is not happy about it. There's not much symbolism or cryptic speech, it's basically a wake-up call where Micah is trying to tell Jerusalem that they are not living right and they are not invincible ... what is happening to the North can (and probably will) happen to them. Remember, in a court of law, some witnesses are better than others.

Micah 5

Not Turning the Other Cheek

*[1] Now you are walled around with a wall; siege is laid against us; with a rod they strike the ruler of Israel upon the
cheek. [2] But you, O Bethlehem of Ephrathah, who are one of the little clans of Judah, from you shall come forth for me
one who is to rule in Israel, whose origin is from of old, from ancient days. [3] Therefore he shall give them up until the
time when she who is in labor has brought forth; then the rest of his kindred shall return to the people of Israel. [4] And he
shall stand and feed his flock in the strength of the LORD, in the majesty of the name of the LORD his God. And they
shall live secure, for now he shall be great to the ends of the earth; [5] and he shall be the one of peace. If the Assyrians
come into our land and tread upon our soil, we will raise against them seven shepherds and eight installed as rulers.*

Choosing Sides

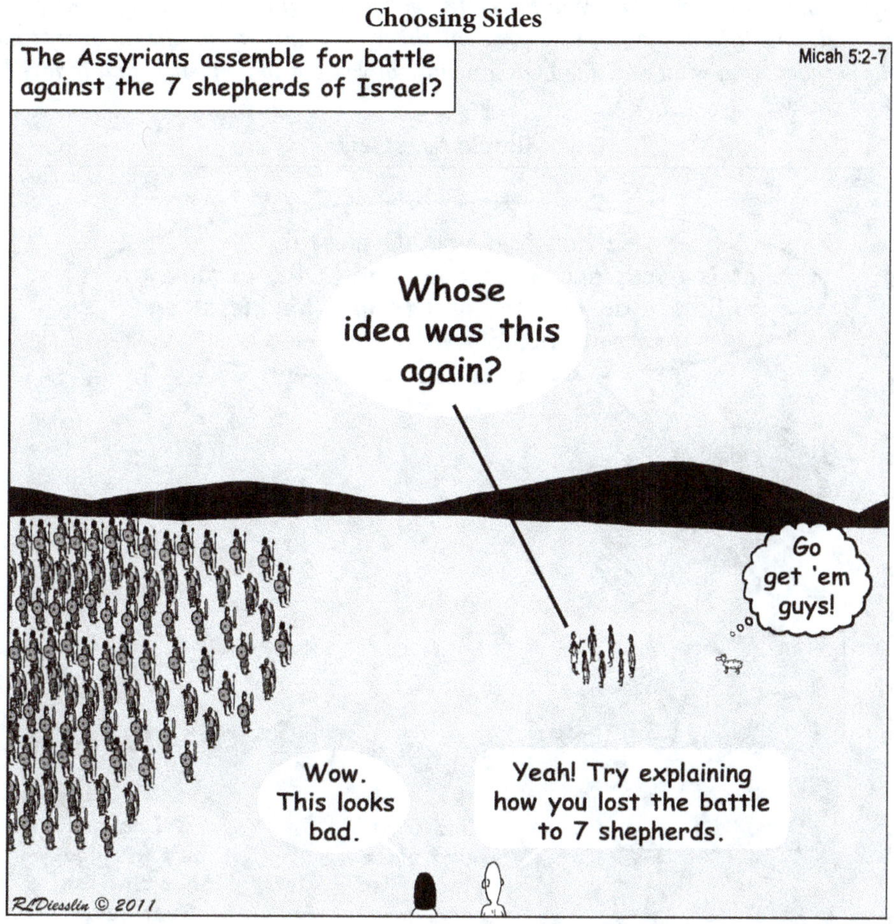

Musings

Now it goes from straight-forward warning to more symbolic hope speech. There's really nowhere to go but up after Assyrian wipes out Jerusalem, so Micah begins to look for hope in the future. Bethlehem's main claim to fame is that it was the city of David, so will salvation come from her again? The prediction never materialized in the short run, although the Persians let the Israelites rebuild Jerusalem, there was to be no kingdom. The symbolism is not lost on Christianity with the ties to Bethlehem, David, kingship and Jesus. Sheep have infinite faith in their shepherds (like dogs to their owners).

Micah 6

Let's Go Over It One More Time

1 Hear what the LORD says: Rise, plead your case before the mountains, and let the hills hear your voice. 2 Hear, you
mountains, the controversy of the LORD, and you enduring foundations of the earth; for the LORD has a controversy
with his people, and he will contend with Israel. 3 "O my people, what have I done to you? In what have I wearied
you? Answer me! 4 For I brought you up from the land of Egypt, and redeemed you from the house of slavery; and I
sent before you Moses, Aaron, and Miriam. 5 O my people, remember now what King Balak of Moab devised, what
Balaam son of Beor answered him, and what happened from Shittim to Gilgal, that you may know the saving acts of
the LORD." 6 "With what shall I come before the LORD, and bow myself before God on high? Shall I come before him
with burnt offerings, with calves a year old? 7 Will the LORD be pleased with thousands of rams, with ten thousands
of rivers of oil? Shall I give my firstborn for my transgression, the fruit of my body for the sin of my soul?" 8 He has told
you, O mortal, what is good; and what does the LORD require of you but to do justice, and to love kindness, and to
walk humbly with your God?

As Simple As It Gets

Musings

Back to the court case God versus the People of Israel, we find God asking what it is they don't seem to remember about their covenant with Moses. Shittim and Gilgal represent the crossing of the Jordan at the end of the Exodus (last camp before the promised land and first camp after entering), thus the fulfilment of the promise to God's people. So what can be done to regain this relationship again now? Clearly no sacrifice, no matter how great, is sufficient. The answer is found in the most famous quote from Micah "*what does the LORD require of you but to do justice, and to love kindness, and to walk humbly with your God?*" (A rhetorical question of course.)

Habakkuk

Habakkuk 1

Wait for It

[1] The oracle that the prophet Habakkuk saw. [2] O LORD, how long shall I cry for help, and you will not listen? Or cry to you "Violence!" and you will not save? [3] Why do you make me see wrongdoing and look at trouble? Destruction and violence are before me; strife and contention arise. [...] [2:1] I will stand at my watchpost, and station myself on the rampart; I will keep watch to see what he will say to me, and what he will answer concerning my complaint. [2] Then the LORD answered me and said: Write the vision; make it plain on tablets, so that a runner may read it. [3] For there is still a vision for the appointed time; it speaks of the end, and does not lie. If it seems to tarry, wait for it; it will surely come, it will not delay. [4] Look at the proud! Their spirit is not right in them, but the righteous live by their faith.

Habakkuk's Very Bad Day

Musings

Chapter 1 poses the question (whiney though it is) to which Chapter 2 provides the answer (the righteous live by their faith). For some reason verse 2:4 was singled out by the Apostle Paul as support for his doctrine of justification by faith, and highly regarded by some Jewish scholars as embodying the entire law (all 613). Personally I just don't see it as all that compelling, but I wasn't consulted.

Zephaniah

Zephaniah 1

“Led Zeppelin” Zephaniah

7 Be silent before the Lord GOD! For the day of the LORD is at hand; the LORD has prepared a sacrifice, he has
consecrated his guests. [...] 12 At that time I will search Jerusalem with lamps, and I will punish the people who rest
complacently on their dregs,
those who say in their hearts,
“The LORD will not do good,
nor will he do harm.” 13 Their
wealth shall be plundered, and
their houses laid waste. Though
they build houses, they shall not
inhabit them; though they plant
vineyards, they shall not drink
wine from them. 14 The great
day of the LORD is near, near
and hastening fast; the sound
of the day of the LORD is bitter,
the warrior cries aloud there. 15
That day will be a day of wrath,
a day of distress and anguish, a
day of ruin and devastation, a
day of darkness and gloom, a
day of clouds and thick dark-
ness, 16 a day of trumpet blast
and battle cry against the forti-
fied cities and against the lofty
battlements. 17 I will bring such
distress upon people that they
shall walk like the blind; be-
cause they have sinned against
the LORD, their blood shall be
poured out like dust, and their
flesh like dung. 18 Neither their
silver nor their gold will be able to save them on the day of the Lord’s wrath; in the fire of his passion the whole earth
shall be consumed; for a full, a terrible end he will make of all the inhabitants of the earth.

Battle of Evermore

Musings

Another “day of the LORD” that sounds like a good day to miss, echoing the concerns of many of the prophets and directed at Judah (in this case). Basically the day of judgment will not be pleasant; the transgressions are many and wealth is not going to be any help in avoiding it. Zephaniah is often pictured as the one carrying the lamp, but it is clearly God who is searching Jerusalem shining the light and exposing both the righteous and the sinner in the process. I couldn’t help but see the imagery from Led Zeppelin’s rock classic “Stairway to Heaven” in this verse.

Zephaniah 3:1-9

Uh Oh - Soiled! or Avoiding a Really Bad Car Pun

1 Ah, soiled, defiled, oppressing city! 2 It has listened to no voice; it has accepted no correction. It has not trusted in the
LORD; it has not drawn near to its God. 3 The officials within it are roaring lions; its judges are evening wolves that
leave nothing until the morning. 4 Its prophets are reckless, faithless persons; its priests have profaned what is sacred,
they have done violence to the law. 5 The LORD within it is righteous; he does no wrong. Every morning he renders his
judgment, each dawn without fail; but the unjust knows no shame. 6 I have cut off nations; their battlements are in
ruins; I have laid waste their streets so that no one walks in them; their cities have been made desolate, without people,
without inhabitants. 7 I said, "Surely the city will fear me, it will accept correction; it will not lose sight of all that I
have brought upon it." But they were the more eager to make all their deeds corrupt. 8 Therefore wait for me, says the
LORD, for the day when I arise as a witness. For my decision is to gather nations, to assemble kingdoms, to pour out
upon them my indignation, all the heat of my anger; for in the fire of my passion all the earth shall be consumed. 9 At
that time I will change the speech of the peoples to a pure speech, that all of them may call on the name of the LORD
and serve him with one accord.

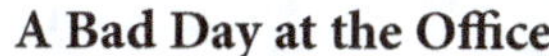

A Bad Day at the Office

Musings

Zephaniah is bringing a familiar warning of doom to Jerusalem, who despite their righteous God, choose evil over good from corrupt government to making a mockery of the law. However, God is not just going to judge Israel but all of the nations. The LORD (YHWH) is shown as worthy and in control of all things that are happening, yet the people reject it (which is much worse than not seeing it). God could continue with the destruction and wipe them all out, but instead decides to be compassionate and purify their speech and have them all serve with one accord.

Zephaniah 3:14-20

Silver Lining

14 Sing aloud, O daughter Zion; shout, O Israel! Rejoice and exult with all your heart, O daughter Jerusalem! 15 The
LORD has taken away the judgments against you, he has turned away your enemies. The king of Israel, the LORD, is
in your midst; you shall fear disaster no more. 16 On that day it shall be said to Jerusalem: Do not fear, O Zion; do not
let your hands grow weak. 17 The LORD, your God, is in your midst, a warrior who gives victory; he will rejoice over
you with gladness, he will renew you in his love; he will exult over you with loud singing 18 as on a day of festival. I will
remove disaster from you, so that you will not bear reproach for it. 19 I will deal with all your oppressors at that time.
And I will save the lame and gather the outcast, and I will change their shame into praise and renown in all the earth.
20 At that time I will bring you home, at the time when I gather you; for I will make you renowned and praised among
all the peoples of the earth, when I restore your fortunes before your eyes, says the LORD.

Needlepoint Prophecy

Musings

And they lived happily ever after! Chapter 3 continues (and ends the short book of Zephaniah) with a very strong note of hope for Jerusalem. The LORD will reverse the current situation and place Israel on the map again in a position of prominence. "*I will change their shame into praise and renown in all the earth*" would clearly be a message of hope for the future. As is often the case, the outcast, the lame, etc., are to be lifted up with the fortunes of the state - the tie to assist those less fortunate within their own society seems ever-present in Hebrew writings! I do not think the rumors of Zephaniah's lucrative needlepoint business have any truth to them (nor was he a member of a rock and roll band) - but hey, the rumors had to start somewhere.

Haggai

Haggai 2

Shake it Baby!

1 In the second year of King Darius, in the seventh month, on the twenty-first day of the month, the word of the LORD
came by the prophet Haggai, saying: 2 Speak now to Zerubbabel son of Shealtiel, governor of Judah, and to Joshua son
of Jehozadak, the high priest, and to the remnant of the people, and say, 3 Who is left among you that saw this house in
its former glory? How does it look to you now? Is it not in your sight as nothing? 4 Yet now take courage, O Zerubbabel,
says the LORD; take courage, O Joshua, son of Jehozadak, the high priest; take courage, all you people of the land,
says the LORD; work, for I am with you, says the LORD of hosts, 5 according to the promise that I made you when you
came out of Egypt. My spirit abides among you; do not fear. 6 For thus says the LORD of hosts: Once again, in a little
while, I will shake the heavens and the earth and the sea and the dry land; 7 and I will shake all the nations, so that the
treasure of all nations shall come, and I will fill this house with splendor, says the LORD of hosts. 8 The silver is mine,
and the gold is mine, says the LORD of hosts. 9 The latter splendor of this house shall be greater than the former, says
the LORD of hosts; and in this place I will give prosperity, says the LORD of hosts.

Name that Tune

Musings

In Chapter 1 Haggai calls on the people to get to work rebuilding the temple ... and they do it! Haggai's book only spans a few months but was apparently a great encouragement to the people. No less here in Chapter 2, Haggai envisions the future glory of the Temple as it is restored and God returns to it. Definitely good news in what was still hard times for the Israelites. Kudos to one of the early motivational speakers of recorded history!

Zechariah

Zechariah 7

Ask a Stupid Question ...

1 In the fourth year of King Darius, the word of the LORD came to Zechariah on the fourth day of the ninth month,
which is Chislev. 2 Now the people of Bethel had sent Sharezer and Regem-melech and their men, to entreat the favor
of the LORD, 3 and to ask the priests of the house of the LORD of hosts and the prophets, "Should I mourn and practice
abstinence in the fifth month, as I have done for so many years?" 4 Then the word of the LORD of hosts came to me: 5
Say to all the people of the land and the priests: When you fasted and lamented in the fifth month and in the seventh,
for these seventy years, was it for me that you fasted? 6 And when you eat and when you drink, do you not eat and
drink only for yourselves? 7 Were not these the words that the LORD proclaimed by the former prophets, when Jeru-
salem was inhabited and in prosperity, along with the towns around it, and when the Negeb and the Shephelah were
inhabited? 8 The word of the LORD came to Zechariah, saying: 9 Thus says the LORD of hosts: Render true judgments,
show kindness and mercy to one another; 10 do not oppress the widow, the orphan, the alien, or the poor; and do not
devise evil in your hearts against one another.

Dude, It's Not that Hard!

Musings

Zechariah and Haggai are contemporaries with a very similar vision of the future restoration of Israel and their writings may have circulated together. Here a group from Bethel arrives in Jerusalem on December 7, 518 B.C.E. and asks about fasting. Zechariah perhaps questions the motive of their visit warning against hypocritical fasting and redirecting the answer toward social kindness and compassion. His answer is pretty much another way of saying the golden rule! Still just as hard to follow today as it was then, and still just as relevant.

Malachi

Malachi 3

Silver and Gold!

[1] See, I am sending my messenger to prepare the way before me, and the Lord whom you seek will suddenly come to his temple. The messenger of the covenant in whom you delight--indeed, he is coming, says the LORD of hosts. [2] But who can endure the day of his coming, and who can stand when he appears? For he is like a refiner's fire and like fullers' soap; [3] he will sit as a refiner and purifier of silver, and he will purify the descendants of Levi and refine them like gold and silver, until they present offerings to the LORD in righteousness. [4] Then the offering of Judah and Jerusalem will be pleasing to the LORD as in the days of old and as in former years.

Better Late Than Never

Musings

Malachi 3:1-4 comes at the end of a long argument between God and the people about God's justice. In the context with this and the post-exilic period in general, Malachi's message is about a messenger who will purify the temple priests and restore worship to it's rightful role. The refining process for metals is used elsewhere in the Old Testament (e.g. Jeremiah 9:7 and Zechariah 13:9) as an analogy for purification. The Christian tradition has also interpreted it messianically with the messenger either being John the Baptist (Mark 1:2 combines this text with Isaiah 40:3 to introduce John the Baptist) or Jesus, hence its use as an Advent reading. In the process prophesying, Malachi comes very close to discovering the formula for a line of best selling self-help books.

Malachi 4

Burn Baby, Burn!

1 See, the day is coming, burning like an oven, when all the arrogant and all evildoers will be stubble; the day that
comes shall burn them up, says the LORD of hosts, so that it will leave them neither root nor branch. 2 But for you
who revere my name the sun of righteousness shall rise, with healing in its wings. You shall go out leaping like calves
from the stall. 3 And you shall tread down the wicked, for they will be ashes under the soles of your feet, on the day
when I act, says the LORD of hosts. 4 Remember the teaching of my servant Moses, the statutes and ordinances that I
commanded him at Horeb for all Israel. 5 Lo, I will send you the prophet Elijah before the great and terrible day of the
LORD comes. 6 He will turn the hearts of parents to their children and the hearts of children to their parents, so that I
will not come and strike the land with a curse.

A Prophet's Job is Never Done

Musings

Malachi weighs in on the day of judgment (or the coming day) with a similar idea of a separation of the good from the bad and the destruction of the bad. He recounts the value of the ten commandments given at Mount Sinai (Horeb) and sees Elijah as the forerunner of that day. Moses and Elijah both experienced the presence of God on Sinai and this idea sort of ties it all together. The New Testament alludes to this as well in Matthew and Mark linking John the Baptist with Elijah and as being the forerunner to the Messiah (aka Jesus). Even though it's not written here, it is upon good authority (okay, silly conjecture) that there were cakes involved (refer back to Elijah).

Baruch

Baruch 5

You're Not Wearing That - Are You!?

1 Take off the garment of your sorrow and affliction, O Jerusalem, and put on forever the beauty of the glory from God.
2 Put on the robe of the righteousness that comes from God; put on your head the diadem of the glory of the Everlasting;
3 for God will show your splendor everywhere under heaven. 4 For God will give you evermore the name, "Righteous
Peace, Godly Glory." 5 Arise, O Jerusalem, stand upon the height; look toward the east, and see your children gathered
from west and east, at the word of the Holy One, rejoicing that God has remembered them. 6 For they went out from
you on foot, led away by their enemies; but God will bring them back to you, carried in glory, as on a royal throne. 7
For God has ordered that every high mountain and the everlasting hills be made low and the valleys filled up, to make
level ground, so that Israel may walk safely in the glory of God. 8 The woods and every fragrant tree have shaded Israel
at God's command. 9 For God will lead Israel with joy, in the light of his glory, with the mercy and righteousness that
come from him.

The Fashion Police

Musings

Baruch was the scribe of the prophet Jeremiah and his writings would be from that same time frame (597 BCE). If you can't find it in your Bible, do not fret. It is an apocryphal book of the Bible (not part of main or original canon of the Bible) and is an optional lectionary reading for that reason. Baruch brings a message of encouragement to the Israelites in exile in Babylon looking forward to the days when they can return to Jerusalem and God will restore them once again. It echoes many of the other prophecies particularly those in Isaiah (40, 43 and 60). Prophets often signal warning in times of prosperity and hope in times of desperation, and this is no exception.

List of Figures

The Cartoon Old Testament

Genesis

Exodus

Leviticus

Numbers

Deuteronomy

Joshua

Ruth

1st Samuel Excerpts

2nd Samuel

1st Kings

2nd Kings

Resources

References

New Revised Standard Version Bible, copyright 1989, Division of Christian Education of the National Council of the Churches of Christ in the United States of America. Used by permission. All rights reserved.

The Torah, A Modern Commentary, edited by Plaut, W. Gunther. New York: Union of American Hebrew Congregations, 1981.

The New Interpreter's Study Bible, New Revised Standard Version with Aprocrypha, edited by Walter J. Harrelson, Abingdon Press, 2003.

Joseph: A Tale of Two Traditions, Author/Cartoonist Richard L. Diesslin, Dayton:DiesslinPress, February, 2007.

The Cartoon Ten Commandments, Author/Cartoonist Richard L. Diesslin, Dayton:DiesslinPress, October, 2000.

Other Books by the Cartoonist

Books in Print:

KNOTS Cartoons, Celebrating the Fun in Scouting, ISBN: 978-0-9702244-8-4 Dayton:Diesslin Press, April 2010, 80p, full color.

A Journey Through Christian Theology, Minneapolis:Fortress Press, ISBN: 978-0-8006969-7-9, March 2010, 2nd Edition. Editor/Author William P. Anderson.

The Cartoon Gospel of John, A Serious Commentary with Visual Parables, ISBN 0-87946-273-6, Chicago:ACTA, September, 2004, p 128. Commentary written by William P. Anderson.

The Cartoon Gospel (of Luke), ISBN 0-940169-09-6, New Berlin:Liturgical Publications, Inc., December, 1990.

E-Books and Cartoon Books and Collections on CD

KNOTS or Not Scouting Cartoon Collection, (these cartoons on CD for newsletters, etc.), ISBN: 978-0-9702244-6-0, and annual supplements.

Joseph: A Tale of Two Traditions, ISBN 0-9702244-7-8, February, 2007.

The Cartoon Ten Commandments, ISBN 0-9702244-2-7, October, 2000.

The Cartoon Gospels, ISBN 0-9702244-5-1, September, 2002.

The Cartoon Gospel of Mark, ISBN 0-9702244-4-3, September, 2002.

The Cartoon Gospel of Matthew, ISBN 0-9702244-3-5, October, 2001.

The Cartoon Gospel (of Luke), ISBN 978-0-9702244-1-5, December, 1990.

Lectionary Readings			
Week	**Sunday**	**Year**	**Old Testament Reading**
1	1st Advent	A	Isaiah 02.01-05
		B	Isaiah 63.16-64.08
		C	Jeremiah 33.14-16
2	2nd Advent	A	Isaiah 11.01-10
		B	Isaiah 40.01-11
		C	Malachi 03.01-04 or
		C	Baruch 05.01-09
3	3rd Advent	A	Isaiah 35.01-10
		B	Isaiah 61.01-04,08-11
		C	Zephaniah 03.14-20
4	4th Advent	A	Isaiah 07.10-15
		B	II Samuel 07.08-16
		C	Micah 05.02-05a(05.01-04a)
5	1st After Christmas	A	Isaiah 63.07-09
		B	Isaiah 61.10-62.03
		C	I Samuel 02.18-20,26
6	2nd After Christmas	AC	Jeremiah 31.07-14
		B	Jeremiah 03.07-14
7	Epiphany	ABC	Isaiah 60.01-06
8	Baptism of the Lord	A	Isaiah 42.01-09
		B	Genesis 01.01-05
		C	Isaiah 61.01-04
9	2nd after Epiphany	A	Isaiah 49.01-07
		B	I Samuel 03.01-10(11-20)
		C	Isaiah 62.01-05
10	3rd after Epiphany	A	Isaiah 09.01-04
		B	Jonah 03.01-05,10
		C	Nehemiah 08.01-04a,05-06,08-10
11	4th after Epiphany	A	Micah 06.01-08
		B	Deuteronomy 18.15-20
		C	Jeremiah 01.04-10
12	5th after Epiphany	A	Isaiah 58.03-09a
		B	Job 07.01-07
		C	Isaiah 06.01-08(09-13)
13	6th after Epiphany	A	Deuteronomy 30.15-20
		B	II Kings 05.01-14
		C	Jeremiah 17.05-10
14	7th after Epiphany	A	Isaiah 49.08-13
		B	Isaiah 43.18-25
		C	Genesis 45.03-11,15

Lectionary Readings (continued)			
Week	**Sunday**	**Year**	**Old Testament Reading**
15	8th after Epiphany	A	Leviticus 19.01-02,09-18
		B	Hosea 02.14-20
		C	Isaiah 55.10-13
16	Last after Epiphany	A	Exodus 24.12-18
		B	II Kings 02.01-12a
		C	Exodus 34.29-35
17	1st of Lent	A	Genesis 02.04b-09,15-17,25-03.07
		B	Genesis 09.08-17
		C	Deuteronomy 26.01-11
18	2nd of Lent	A	Genesis 12.01-04a(04b-08)
		B	Genesis 17.01-10,15-19
		C	Genesis 15.01-12
19	3rd of Lent	A	Exodus 17.03-07
		B	Exodus 20.01-17
		C	Exodus 03.01-15
20	Forth of Lent	A	I Samuel 16.01-13
		B	II Chronicles 36.14-23
		C	Joshua 05.09-12
21	5th of Lent	A	Ezekiel 37.01-14
		B	Jeremiah 31.31-34
		C	Isaiah 43.16-21
22	6th of Lent	ABC	Isaiah 50.04-09a
23	Easter Sunday	A	Jeremiah 31:01-06
		B	Isaiah 25.06-09
		C	Isaiah 65.17-25
30	Pentecost	A	Numbers 11:24-30
		B	Ezekiel 37.01-14
		C	Genesis 11.01-09
31	Trinity Sunday	A	Deuteronomy 04.32-40
		B	Isaiah 06.01-08
		C	Proverbs 08.22-31
32	5/29 - 6/4	A	Genesis 12.01-09
		B	I Samuel 16.01-13
		C	I Kings 08.22-23,41-43
33	6/5-11	A	Genesis 22.01-18
		B	I Samuel 16.14-23
		C	I Kings 17.17-24
34	6/12-18	A	Genesis 25.19-34
		B	II Samuel 01.01,17-27
		C	I Kings 19.01-08

Lectionary Readings (continued)			
Week	**Sunday**	**Year**	**Old Testament Reading**
35	6/19-25	A	Genesis 28.10-17
		B	II Samuel 05.01-12
		C	I Kings 19.09-14
36	6/26-7/2	A	Genesis 32.22-32
		B	II Samuel 06.01-15
		C	I Kings 19.15-21
37	7/3-9	A	Exodus 01.06-14,22-02.10
		B	II Samuel 07.01-17
		C	I Kings 21.01-02,17-21
38	7/10-16	A	Exodus 02.11-22
		B	II Samuel 07.18-29
		C	II Kings 02.01,06-14
39	7/17-23	A	Exodus 03.01-12
		B	II Samuel 11.01-15
		C	II Kings 04.08-17
40	7/24-30	A	Exodus 03.13-20
		B	II Samuel 12.01-14
		C	II Kings 05.01-05ab
41	7/31-8/6	A	Exodus 12.01-14
		B	II Samuel 12.15b-24
		C	II Kings 13.14-20a
42	8/7-13	A	Exodus 14.19-31
		B	II Samuel 18.01,05,09-15
		C	Jeremiah 18.01-11
43	8/14-20	A	Exodus 16.02-15
		B	II Samuel 18.24-33
		C	Jeremiah 20.01-13
44	8/21-27	A	Exodus 17.01-07
		B	II Samuel 23.01-07
		C	Jeremiah 28.01-09
45	8/28-9/3	A	Exodus 19.01-09
		B	I Kings 02.01-04,10-12
		C	Ezekiel 18.01-09,25-29
46	9/4-10	A	Exodus 19.16-24
		B	Proverbs 02.01-08
		C	Ezekiel 33.01-11
47	9/11-17	A	Exodus 20.01-20
		B	Proverbs 22.01-02;08-09
		C	Hosea 04.01-03,05.15-06.06

Lectionary Readings (concluded)			
Week	**Sunday**	**Year**	**Old Testament Reading**
48	9/18-24	A	Exodus 32.01-14
		B	Job 28.20
		C	Hosea 11.01-11
49	9/25-10/1	A	Exodus 33.12-23
		B	Job 42.01-06
		C	Joel 02.23-30
50	10/2-8	A	Numbers 27.12-23
		B	Genesis 02.18-24
		C	Amos 05.06-07,10-15
51	10/9-15	A	Deuteronomy 34.01-12
		B	Genesis 03.08-19
		C	Micah 01.02,02.01-10
52	10/16-22	A	Ruth 01.01-19a
		B	Isaiah 53.07-12
		C	Habakkuk 01.01-03,02.01-04
53	10/23-29	A	Ruth 02.01-13
		B	Jeremiah 31.07-09
		C	Zephaniah 03.01-09
54	10/30-11/5	A	Ruth 04.07-17
		B	Deuteronomy 06.01-09
		C	Haggai 02.01-09
55	11/6-12	A	Amos 05.18-24
		B	I Kings 17.08-16
		C	Zechariah 07.01-10
56	11/13-19	A	Zephaniah 01.07,12-18
		B	Dan 07.09-14
		C	Malachi 04.01-06
57	11/20-26	A	Ezekiel 34.11-16,20-24
		B	Jeremiah 23.01-06
		C	II Samuel 05.01-05

www.ingramcontent.com/pod-product-compliance
Lightning Source LLC
Chambersburg PA
CBHW080447030726
47592CB00011B/3012

9780984887200